Homestyle ITALIAN Cooking

BY
LORI CARANGELO

THE CROSSING PRESS
FREEDOM, CALIFORNIA

CONTENTS

PREFACE

I went to Italy to search for my roots. Somehow, all of my research steered me to food, because Italians love to cook and share good food. While researching my grandfather's birthplace, Dolceacqua, Liguria, I found my relatives and was wined and dined beyond my wildest culinary fantasies.

Upon visiting my grandmother's birthplace on the Amalfi Coast in southern Italy's Campania region, I collected recipes for their world famous pizzas and pastas. Everywhere I traveled, I collected recipes. When I returned home I had more than an appreciation of my ancestors and the lives they led. I came home with the basis for this book.

The Italian cooking I love is firmly rooted in the land. Even in the most cosmopolitan Roman restaurant, the menu is based on the classic cuisine of simple farmers' kitchens.

The recipes in this book are the same as those carefully prepared in the neighborhood trattoria each night—the sort of place that has a menu always posted in the front window or just inside the door, next to a sign that reads "*Produzione Propria*," which means homemade.

The recipes remind me of the numerous times I ended a day with a relaxing meal at a local trattoria. I always tried to sample the best eating of each region—*tagliatelle con pesto* in Genoa, *lasagna verdi* in Bologna, *bistecca alla Fiorentina* in Florence, *saltimbocca* in Rome, pizza in Naples, all accompanied by local wines. More often than not, the food was simple, honest, and appealing. There were no mysterious sauces to mask the flavor of carefully prepared fresh food. I hope you'll have the opportunity to sample these wonderful dishes in your own kitchen.

The process of translation in this collection was often difficult. It was not so much due to the language barrier, but to the Italians' indifference to precise measurements. My Italian grandmother created gastronomic wonders with a handful of this and a pinch of that, and so do many master chefs. They are guided by feel, not by the measuring cup. One comes to know, from the love of cooking, how much will feed how many, how much is enough to create the desired flavor and result. But for the novice, I have translated and elaborated upon nearly all the recipes contained here. Don't be afraid to approximate; it's very difficult to ruin an Italian dish. The result depends upon the excellence of the ingredients, which varies from one tomato to the next. Therefore, the same recipe may not turn out exactly the same every time. The amount of sauce, the number of servings—it's all up to you and your guests.

INGREDIENTS IN ITALIAN COOKING

If your only exposure to Italian cooking has been in those Italian-American restaurants where every dish is smothered in a heavily spiced tomato sauce, you may have the wrong idea of what Italian cooking is all about. Italian cooking is about fresh ingredients, carefully prepared to bring out the essential flavor and character of the ingredients at hand.

Most of the ingredients called for in this cookbook are readily available in supermarkets in the States.

Here is a listing and discussions of some of the ingredients you'll want to have on hand.

GARLIC AND ONIONS

Pliny, the Roman historian, lists 61 medicinal uses for garlic. It is said to cure colds, warts, fainting spells, and insect and snake bites. It is said to stop vampires, improve circulation, alleviate high blood pressure, ward off the evil eye, repel fleas, and cause hair to grow.

A number of folk sayings indicate the importance of garlic and onions in Italian cuisine: "Peace and happiness begin when garlic is used in cooking," and "Banish garlic from the kitchen and the pleasure of eating flies with it."

A fundamental procedure in a vast number of Italian dishes is sautéing onion or garlic or both in hot fat before adding other ingredients. This provides a background flavor, which may be faint or pronounced, sweet or pungent, depending on how lightly or deeply the onion and garlic are browned.

Garlic colors more quickly than onion, so if a recipe calls for both, sauté the onion first, then when the onion becomes a light gold color add the garlic. The stronger or darker the browning, the stronger the flavor. Garlic gives all its flavor to the sauce when it is cut so finely it is almost mashed. Removing the tiny green germ in the center of the clove before cooking will eliminate the strong garlic smell if that is objectionable to you.

HERBS AND SPICES

Beyond onion and garlic, several herbs and spices, all readily available in the United States, lend flavor to Italian dishes. Here is a listing of them.

Basil (*Basilico*)

A member of the mint family, basil has a distinctive, spicy aroma. Fresh, it may very well be the best of all herbs to use to flavor tomatoes and tomato sauce. In Italian cooking it is associated with the region of Liguria, the home of pesto–the aromatic paste of basil, olive oil, Parmesan cheese, garlic, and pine nuts. Basil retains the most flavor when it is cut and added to a dish at the last moment. The fresh leaves can be preserved by covering with oil (preferably olive oil) in a lidded jar and refrigerating or freezing. Dried basil loses a good deal of its pungency.

Bay Leaf (Lauro)

A native of the Mediterranean, the stiff green leaves were used to crown Olympic champions. Today, the bay laurel leaf is used to flavor soups, casseroles, stews, and roasts. The leaf is usually removed before the dish is served.

Cinnamon (Cannella)

This ancient spice is used primarily in sweet dishes, but is occasionally added to meat and garnishes.

Fennel (Finocchio)

Fennel is grown extensively throughout Italy. A member of the carrot family, the bulb of this plant has an anise flavor and is used whole or sliced, as a cooked vegetable or raw in salads. The leaves are used in sauces, mayonnaise, and egg and fish dishes. The seeds flavor sausages, cooked meats, dried figs, and cookies.

Italian Parsley (Prezzemolo)

This is a flat-leafed variety used to flavor soups, stews, and salads. It is also used as a garnish for many dishes. It is milder in flavor than the curly leaf parsley familiar to most Americans.

Marjoram (Maggiorana)

Closely related to oregano, marjoram is a sweet, aromatic herb used in soups, stews, and vegetable and fish dishes.

Mint (Menta)

Used with vegetables, soups, salads, fish, and fowl, mint should be used sparingly since it is very aromatic. Mint is characteristic of the cooking of southern Italy, which was influenced by the cooking of the Middle East.

Nutmeg (Noce Moscata)

A pinch of nutmeg is used to flavor spinach, mushrooms, ravioli, and cheese dishes. Nutmeg is always freshly grated in Italian cooking. Packaged ground nutmeg cannot compare in flavor and aroma.

Oregano (Origano)

This herb, the wild variety of marjoram, is most closely associated with Italian cooking in America. The unmistakable flavor of oregano is found in pizza, sauces, and casseroles. Oregano is one of the few herbs that does not lose its flavor when dried.

Pepper (Pepe)

The popularity of peppercorns in northern Europe made the spice merchants of Venice and Genoa quite rich. Black and white peppercorns come from the same berry; the white is picked when the berry is almost ripe, the black is picked when the berry is still unripe. Both are then dried. Black peppercorns have the stronger flavor, but white is preferable for some dishes because of its color.

Rosemary (Rosmario)

A perennial shrub that grows wild by the sea, rosemary has leaves that resemble small needles. It is used most often with roasted meats, particularly lamb, chicken, and pork. This is a very aromatic herb and should be used sparingly.

Saffron *(Zafferano)*

Saffron lends a distinctive flavor and yellow color to foods. Saffron is very expensive as it is the collected pollen of the crocus flower. Something like 40,000 flowers are required to make 1 pound of the spice. It is available as a powder or in threads (the stigmas of the flower). The most economical way to use saffron is to steep threads in tepid water for a few minutes, strain and add the liquid to the dish for color and taste. *Risotto alla Milanese* is a classic dish enhanced by saffron.

Sage *(Salvia)*

Once established in a garden, this herb blooms year after year. A member of the mint family, sage is used to flavor veal, liver, and sausage.

Salt *(Sale)*

The salt generally used in Italy is sea salt, extracted from evaporated sea water. The fruity flavor improves the simplest dish. Sea salt can be obtained in many supermarkets, as well as in natural foods stores.

When adding salt, bear in mind that some of the ingredients already present, or to be added later in the dish, may be salty. This is often the case with sauces for pasta. Romano sprinkled on top of a spaghetti dinner adds salt to the dish; commercial brands of Parmesan are saltier than either fresh Parmesan or fresh Romano. If the sauce contains prosciutto, sausages, anchovies, capers, or cheese, you may need to hold back some of the salt you add to the water in which you boil the pasta. But understand that adding salt to pasta at the table is seldom as effective as adding salt to the water in which the pasta was cooked.

Prolonged contact with salt draws out moisture—you may want to do this sometimes, as when cooking eggplant, but you definitely do not want to lose any precious moisture from veal scaloppini, chicken breasts, or thin slices of beef. In sautéing these, do not add any salt until they are almost completely cooked.

Salted batter diminishes the crispness of deep-fried foods, but totally unsalted fried food can never be adequately corrected at the table.

In many recipes, lemon juice is the perfect substitute for salt, especially for people on salt-restricted diets.

Thyme *(Timo)*

This easy-to-grow herb with its mint-like aroma is used in stuffings, soups, casseroles, and beans.

Vanilla *(Vaniglia)*

To flavor desserts, keep a vanilla bean in sugar to give additional flavor.

ITALIAN CHEESES

Italians have been making cheese for thousands of years. The cheese that comes from the Alps is very different from the cheese from the Po Valley, the Abruzzi, or from the hot South. There is creamy Bel Paese, and blue-striped Gorgonzola. There is sharp sheep's cheese which is made from whey and, when freshly grated, is used to perk up soups, sauces, and pasta dishes.

The following cheeses are available in the U.S. in Italian markets and specialty food stores, if not at your supermarket.

Asiago

This cheese dates back to the Middle Ages, though it was scarcely known outside of the Veneto region until relatively recently. When young, asiago is a semi-soft slicing cheese, great for pastas and pizza. Aged asiago can be grated and is sometimes used as a substitute for Parmesan cheese by those watching their diets.

Bel Paese

A semi-soft, very mild cheese made from cow's milk. It is used as a table cheese, but its melting qualities make it suitable for cooking.

Caciocavallo

Similar to provolone cheese. It originally came from the southern provinces but is now also made in northern Italy. It is mild, has a spicy tang when young, and is used mostly as a table cheese, although it hardens as it matures and can then be grated.

Fontina

A fairly firm cheese, similar to Gruyère in texture, but having tiny holes on the surface. Not only is it indispensable in preparing fondue, but it is an excellent table cheese. The taste is slightly sweet, with a nutty flavor. Don't confuse Italian fontina with Danish fontina; the two are not really similar.

Gorgonzola

This rich, creamy, blue-green veined cheese made from whole cow's milk can be mild (*dolce*) or sharp (*piccante*). It is used as a table cheese and is particularly tasty over pasta.

Mascarpone

This rich, fresh cream cheese spreads easily. For a dessert it can be sprinkled with sugar and/or cocoa powder. In this country, mascarpone is used in tiramisu, which is made with sponge cake soaked in brandy and espresso and layered with a mascarpone custard.

Mozzarella

Originally made from water buffalo milk, most mozzarella is presently made from cow's milk, although some buffalo milk mozzarella can be found in Italian specialty food shops. A bland, smooth cheese, it is prized for its melting qualities in lasagna, pizza, and other baked dishes; sliced cold in salads and sandwiches, it has a mild, nutty flavor. Fresh mozzarella is far superior to packaged cheese. Fresh mozzarella should be used within 2 to 3 days after purchasing. Smoked mozzarella keeps a bit longer.

Parmesan *(Parmigiano)*

Made from cow's milk, good Parmesan is straw-colored, crumbly, and mellow but salty in flavor. The best and most expensive is Parmigiano-Reggiano from Parma, Italy. Aged Parmesan is grated and served over pasta, in soups, salads, and many other dishes; it is best when freshly grated. In Italy, when this cheese is very fresh and moist, it is eaten as a table cheese.

Pecorino

This medium sharp cheese is made from sheep's milk or goat's milk. Pecorino Romano, a hard cheese that is aged for 8 months, is used alone in dishes or combined with Parmesan.

Provolone

A hard, but creamy, cheese made from cow's milk, provolone can be mild or sharp, fresh or smoked. It melts easily and can be grated or sliced.

Ricotta

Ricotta resembles a smooth cottage cheese and can be made from either cow's or goat's milk. Actually it isn't made from fresh milk at all; ricotta is made from whey, the liquid byproduct of cheese production. Fresh ricotta is used in cooking, but it can also be a table cheese; it is used as a filling of both pasta and pastries, including cannoli.

MEATS

Many of the recipes call for prosciutto as a flavoring agent. This is a very delicately flavored, high-quality cured ham. There are several different types of prosciutto. All are cured with a similar formula, but aged for varying lengths of time. The prosciutto considered best is from Parma (Parma hams). The young pigs are raised on whey, a byproduct of Parmesan cheese. Only recently has the U.S. government allowed Italian prosciutto to be imported into this country after a ban of 20 years. (There were questions about the meat's safety as an uncooked product.) Look for it in specialty food stores and expect to pay a premium price.

Pancetta is often referred to as Italian bacon. It looks similar to American bacon, but the flavor of this cured and air-dried meat is different. Pancetta can be used instead of prosciutto in a recipe.

OIL

It's hard to imagine Italian cooking without olive oil. When added to a dish, it supplies a marvelous fruity fragrance.

There are several grades of olive oil. The finest olive oils, with the richest flavor and aroma and the deepest green coloring are virgin olive oils. Virgin olive oil is extracted from the first pressing of olives. There is extra virgin olive oil, with a maximum acidity of 1 percent; superfine virgin olive, fine virgin olive oil, and virgin olive oil have increasing amounts of acidity (up to 3.5 percent). These oils are all suitable for using in dishes that require no cooking. Pure olive oil is a blend of refined oil and virgin oil, and it is suitable for use in cooking.

FLOUR

Most of the recipes in this book require all-purpose flour, even the recipes for making pasta. Although good dried pasta is made from semolina flour or durum wheat, fresh pasta is lighter and richer because it contains eggs. So fresh pasta is usually made with all-purpose flour, which contains a percentage of hard wheat (durum) flour.

A few recipes call for a soft Italian flour. For these recipes, use cake flour or pastry flour. If you use all-purpose flour, use a little less flour than the recipe suggests.

ANTIPASTI

▲▲▲▲▲▲▲▲▲▲▲▲▲▲▲▲▲

Antipasto, literally "before the meal" (not "before the pasta," as it is often translated), is a starter served before the main dish. There are some restaurants famed for their antipasti tables that offer as many as 60 dishes to tantalize your palate. Although an antipasto dish is usually considered to be an appetizer, many antipasti are generous enough to make an entire meal, by American standards.

ANTIPASTO COMBINATIONS

Calamari al Pesto—Squid with pesto

Calamari Ripieni—Stuffed squid

Capitone sotto Aceto—Eels in marinade

Caponata all Siciliana—Eggplant relish

Carciofi alla Romana—Artichokes, Roman style

Carciofi Ripieni—Stuffed artichokes

Carciofini—Artichoke hearts

Cipolle Ripieni—Stuffed onions

Cipolline alla Zaferano—Pearl onions in saffron

Cozze en Salsa Verde—Mussels in green sauce

Fagiole con Peperoni—Beans with sweet peppers

Funghi al Limone—Pickled mushrooms

Funghi Marinata—Marinated mushrooms

Funghi Ripieni—Stuffed mushrooms

Giardiniera—Pickled vegetable salad

Melanzane Marinate—Marinated eggplant

Muscoli alla Marinara—Mussels in marinara sauce

Peperoni Rossi Ripieni—Stuffed red bell peppers

Peperoni Verdi Ripieni—Stuffed green bell peppers

Petto di Vitello Farcito—Stuffed breast of veal

Prosciutto e Melone—Italian ham and melon

Pomodori con Olive—Tomatoes with olives

Pomodori Ripieni—Stuffed tomatoes

Scampi all'Aglio—Shrimp in garlic sauce

Scarola Ripieni—Stuffed escarole

Torta Rustica di Carne—Small meat pie, country-style

Trippa alla Friuliana—Tripe, Friuli style

Trippa di Borgataro—Tripe, Borgataro style

Trotta en Carpione—Pickled trout

Vongole all'Oregano—Clams with oregano

Zucchini Fritti—Fried zucchini

Zucchini Ripieni—Stuffed zucchini

Zucchini Scapece—Minted zucchini

OTHER ANTIPASTI

Bruschetta—Thick slices of toasted bread seasoned with garlic, oil, salt, and pepper.

Carpaccio—Very thin medallions of raw beef arrayed on a platter, lightly glossed with olive oil, and decorated with anchovy fillets, roasted slivers of green pepper, and scatterings of capers.

Crostini—Fingers of bread baked with mozzarella, anchovies, tomato, oregano, salt, and pepper.

Spiedini—Cheese skewers (usually mozzarella, bread, and anchovies).

SINGLE INGREDIENTS

SAUSAGES

Cappocollo—Smoked pork

Chipolata—Small pork and rice sausages ("little fingers")

Mortadella—Original Bolognese pork sausage flavored with peppercorns, pistachios, wine, sugar, and olives. This smooth mix (pounded in a mortar, hence its name) is what has come to be known as bologna or baloney

Salsicca secca—Dry and peppery pork sausage

HAM

Prosciutto—Thin-sliced, raw cured ham

SALAMI

Various salt-cured pork sausages. Salami are made throughout Italy; the seasonings, sizes, and smoothness of the grind varies from region to region.

Calabrese—A red hot salami from southern Italy

Campagnole—a rough-textured, spicy, peasant salami

Cotechino—Large, cooked pork salami

Cotto—Soft, cooked sandwich-size salami

Genoa—Veal and pork seasoned salami

Milano—Beef and pork seasoned salami

Pepperoni—Small dry salami-like sausage, sweet or hot

Soppressata—Oval, flat salami; peppery, gingery, very garlicky in flavor

VEGETABLES

Caponata, any dried bean or chick-pea salad, marinated or pickled beets or artichoke hearts, green or ripe olives, radishes, celery or carrots, fennel or celery hearts, pickled hot green or red peppers, pimientos in oil, cherry tomatoes.

CHEESES

Provolone, mozzarella, and gorgonzola are cheeses featured in antipasto dishes.

Carciofi alla Venezia Giulia

VENETIAN ARTICHOKES

SERVES 6

The artichokes for this recipe must be young; they should not yet have formed a choke.

INGREDIENTS

16 small artichokes	2 to 3 sprigs parsley, finely chopped
Juice of 1 lemon	1 cup olive oil
6 to 8 tablespoons fresh bread crumbs	Salt and pepper to taste
1 garlic clove, minced	

METHOD

■ Prepare each artichoke by cutting off the stalk (the artichoke should stand easily on its base) and by trimming off the tough lower leaves. Carefully open out the remaining leaves. Soak the artichokes with the lemon juice and water to cover for 15 minutes.

■ Combine the bread crumbs, garlic, parsley, and 2 to 3 tablespoons of the olive oil to make a stuffing. Season with salt and pepper.

■ Drain the artichokes and push the stuffing in between the leaves. Arrange the artichokes upright in a pan just large enough to hold them. Pour over the remaining oil, and add enough water to come halfway up the sides of the artichokes. Cover the pan, bring the water to a boil, and simmer until the artichokes are tender, about 30 minutes. Add more water if necessary during the cooking. Remove the artichokes from the water, drain, and serve hot.

Pane con Formaggio

BREAD WITH CHEESE

SERVES 4

INGREDIENTS

1/2 cup butter	1 to 2 cups freshly grated mozzarella cheese
1 teaspoon minced garlic	
1 small loaf French bread	4 teaspoons chopped fresh basil

METHOD

■ Preheat the oven to 450° F.

■ In a small saucepan, melt the butter. Add the garlic and gently simmer for about 2 minutes.

■ Slice the bread in half horizontally; then cut each half into 4 to 6 pieces. Brush each piece of bread with the garlic butter and arrange on a baking sheet. Sprinkle with grated mozzarella and basil. Toast in the oven for 3 to 5 minutes, or until the cheese is melted and bubbly. Serve hot.

Fagiolo Toscanelli al Caviale

TUSCAN BEANS WITH CAVIAR

SERVES 4

INGREDIENTS

1/2 pound dry white beans	1 tablespoon caviar
3/4 cup extra virgin olive oil	1/3 cup fresh lemon juice
2 large garlic cloves, minced	Salt and pepper to taste
1 teaspoon chopped fresh sage	

METHOD

■ Soak the beans overnight in water to cover by 2 inches. The next day drain the beans and add fresh water, covering the beans by 2 inches. Bring the beans to a boil and simmer until tender. Rinse and add the olive oil, garlic, sage, caviar, lemon juice, and salt and pepper. Mix gently. Marinate for at least 30 minutes before serving. Serve at room temperature.

Parmesan Pie with Truffles

**SERVES
6 TO 8**

In the autumn, truffles (tartufi) are plentiful in northern Italy where this recipe originated.

INGREDIENTS

White truffles, thinly sliced

Parmesan cheese (aged less than 1 year), diced

Olive oil

METHOD

■ Heat the oven to 350° F.

■ Grease a baking dish. Cover the bottom with a single layer of truffles. Add a layer of Parmesan, another layer of truffles, and a final layer of Parmesan. Sprinkle with olive oil and bake for a few minutes, just long enough to soften the cheese and bind it with the truffles.

POLENTA WITH TRUFFLES AND PARMESAN

Start with a layer of polenta, then alternate layers of truffles and Parmesan.

Panzarotti

FRIED CHEESE-STUFFED RAVIOLI

SERVES 6

INGREDIENTS

FILLING

1 cup diced fresh mozzarella cheese

2 eggs

5 tablespoons grated Parmesan cheese

Salt to taste

1/4 pound salami or Parma ham (prosciutto), diced (optional)

RAVIOLI

2 1/2 cups all-purpose flour

1/2 cup olive oil

2 egg yolks

Salt

Vegetable oil for frying

METHOD

■ To make the filling, combine the mozzarella in a bowl with the eggs, Parmesan, salt, and salami. Mix thoroughly. Set aside while you make the dough.

■ To make the dough, sift the flour into a mound on a pastry board or into a bowl. Make a well in the center. Add the oil, a pinch of salt, the egg yolks, and about 1 tablespoon lukewarm water. Mix well. Knead to a firm dough. If the dough is too dry, add water; if too wet, add flour. When it is smooth and elastic, put it in a lightly floured bowl, cover, and allow to rest for about 30 minutes. Roll the dough into a thin sheet; then cut it into circles about 2 1/2 inches in diameter. Put a teaspoon of the filling mixture on each circle of dough, fold the circle in half, and seal the edges with a fork.

■ Deep fry the panzarotti a few at a time until crisp and golden brown. Drain. Serve very hot.

Fried Mozzarella Marinara

SERVES 2 TO 4

INGREDIENTS

1 cup dry bread crumbs	1 egg, beaten
Salt and pepper to taste	1/3 cup all-purpose flour
1/2 cup grated Parmesan cheese, divided	Vegetable oil
1/2 pound mozzarella cheese, cut in pieces 3 inches by 2 inches by 1/2 inch	Approximately 1 cup Marinara Sauce (see page 41)

METHOD

■ Mix the bread crumbs with the salt and pepper and 2 tablespoons of the Parmesan cheese.

■ Dip the cheese slices into the beaten egg, then into the flour, then into the seasoned bread crumbs, turning to coat all sides. Place the pieces of breaded cheese in a single layer on a plate and chill for 30 minutes.

■ Heat 1/2 inch of oil in a large, heavy pan. Fry the cheese pieces until lightly browned on one side, then turn and brown on the other side. Take care not to overcook or the cheese will toughen. Drain the cheese pieces on paper towels.

■ Serve the fried mozzarella with a dish of heated Marinara Sauce for dipping and the rest of the Parmesan cheese for sprinkling.

Verze Ripiene

STUFFED CABBAGE

SERVES 8 TO 10

INGREDIENTS

1 large cabbage (savoy is recommended)	1/4 teaspoon dried oregano
1 pound ground pork	2 1/2 teaspoons salt, divided
1 cup cooked white rice	3/4 teaspoon freshly ground black pepper, divided
1/2 cup chopped onions	
1/4 cup chopped fresh parsley	3 cups tomato purée
1/2 cup grated Romano or Parmesan cheese	1 bay leaf

METHOD

■ Wash the cabbage, place it in a large pot, and cover with water. Bring to a boil; then simmer for 10 minutes. Drain. Let the cabbage stand until it is cool enough to handle. Remove 24 large leaves.

■ Mix together the pork, rice, onions, parsley, cheese, oregano, 1 1/2 teaspoons of the salt, and 1/2 teaspoon of the pepper. Place a heaping teaspoon of the mixture on each leaf, turn in the sides, and carefully roll up. (If any meat mixture is left over, make more rolls or make meatballs.)

■ Preheat the oven to 350° F. Arrange the rolls in a greased casserole or baking dish. Add the tomato sauce, the remaining salt and pepper, and the bay leaf. Cover and bake for 1 1/2 hours. Taste for seasoning, discard the bay leaf, and serve hot.

Scarole Ripieni

STUFFED ESCAROLE

SERVES 6 TO 8

INGREDIENTS

2 cups fresh bread crumbs	2 tablespoons pine nuts
1/4 cup grated Romano cheese	1 tablespoon chopped fresh parsley
1/4 cup grated Parmesan cheese	Dash pepper
2 garlic cloves, minced, divided	2 small heads escarole
2 tablespoons raisins	1 tablespoon olive oil

METHOD

■ To make the stuffing, combine the bread crumbs, Romano cheese, Parmesan cheese, 1 clove minced garlic, raisins, pine nuts, parsley, and pepper in a mixing bowl. Set aside.

■ Leaving the heads intact, spread the leaves of the escarole gently and wash thoroughly. Turn each head upside down and drain well. Open the head, spreading the leaves until the center is exposed. Place half the stuffing in the center of each head. Bring the escarole leaves up over the filling and tie with string.

■ In a large saucepan, heat the olive oil. Add the remaining minced garlic and sauté until golden. Add 1 cup of water and the escarole. Cover tightly and cook over medium heat for about 8 minutes. Turn the escarole over. Cook, covered, for 5 more minutes or until the escarole is tender.

■ To serve, slice the escarole crosswise.

ITALIAN SOUPS

▲▲▲▲▲▲▲▲▲▲▲▲▲▲▲▲▲

The Italian cook's repertoire includes a rich assortment of soups. The lighter, less filling soups (*minestra*) with a clear broth base (*broda*) make an excellent first course. Sometimes the broth base will be slightly thickened with egg and perhaps grated Parmesan cheese. The distinct shapes of the vegetables and pasta or rice are retained in these soups.

For a lunch or dinner entrée, there are the more substantial soups (*zuppa*), brimming with meat, poultry, fish, or vegetables. Often these are served ladled over a piece of bread or toast. This tradition has its roots in medieval times, when servants made soups from the leavings of the aristocrats. In those days, large slices of bread were used instead of plates to hold food—so the plates, ladened with leftovers, were tossed into the pot, along with water and herbs. The result: zuppa!

Minestrone alla Genovese

MINESTRONE SOUP, GENOA-STYLE

**SERVES
10 TO 12**

This soup is a classic: a green minestrone in a clear soup base. The color comes from the addition of pesto at the last moment.

INGREDIENTS

1 pound ham	1 pound green beans, in 2-inch pieces
1 pound chicken parts (wings, backs, neck)	1/2 cup uncooked ditalini
1/4 pound sliced prosciutto	1 cup fresh or frozen peas
2 cups peeled and diced potato	3 to 4 cups shredded cabbage
2 cups sliced celery	About 2 tablespoons salt
4 small zucchini, diced	1 cup Pesto (see page 43)
1/2 cup sliced leeks	

METHOD

■ In a large kettle, combine 4 quarts water, the ham, chicken, and prosciutto, and bring to a boil. Reduce the heat, cover, and simmer for 10 minutes. Add the celery, zucchini, leeks, green beans, and ditalini. Simmer, uncovered, for 4 to 5 minutes. Add salt to taste.

■ To serve, pour the soup into individual bowls. Top each serving with a generous dollop of pesto.

Zuppa Francesa

SERVES 1

An old dish cooked by Franciscan Friars in the 1800s.

INGREDIENTS

1 tomato	Salt to taste
2 garlic cloves, divided	Pinch dried thyme
1 tablespoon olive oil	1 egg yolk
1 teaspoon minced fresh parsley	4 slices toasted bread
6 fresh basil leaves	

METHOD

■ Dip the tomato into boiling water for about 10 seconds. Cool and peel. Make a cut at the bottom of the tomato, and wedge in 1 clove of garlic.

■ Heat the olive oil and parsley in a saucepan until the oil turns golden brown, about 3 minutes. Add the tomato and fry it for 2 minutes; then pour some water into the saucepan to almost cover the tomato. Add the basil and salt, and let simmer for about 10 minutes. Remove the saucepan from the heat, and add the thyme and the egg yolk.

■ Rub the toast with the remaining garlic clove. Serve the toast with the soup.

Zuppa di Pesce

FISH SOUP

SERVES 4

Each region of Italy has its own version of fish stew (in French, bouill-abaisse), often made with less expensive varieties of fish. Zuppa di Pesce always includes two or more kinds of fish, squid, or shellfish.

INGREDIENTS

2 pounds mixed fish and shellfish: shrimp (shelled); squid (cleaned and skinned), mussels (scrubbed and debearded); red snapper, etc.	2 onions, sliced
	2 garlic cloves
	2 tablespoons chopped fresh parsley
2 tablespoons olive oil	1 tablespoon tomato paste
1/2 cup white wine	2 tablespoons white wine vinegar
	Salt and pepper to taste

METHOD

■ Slice the squid in rings. Cut the fish into pieces.

■ Warm the oil in a heavy saucepan. Add the squid rings and fry for several minutes. Add the wine and continue to cook over slow heat. When the squid looks nearly cooked, add the shellfish, mussels, and fish pieces and simmer for another 2 minutes.

■ With a slotted spoon, remove all the fish and shellfish to a serving bowl. To the remaining juices in the pan, add the sliced onions, garlic, and parsley, and let them "sweat" for a few minutes. Then add the tomato paste and 1/4 cup warm water, and simmer for 40 minutes. Return the fish to the pot and add the vinegar. Season with salt and pepper and simmer for 10 minutes. Serve immediately, or cool and refrigerate the soup for reheating later.

Zuppa di Pesce alla Barese

FISH SOUP, BARI-STYLE

SERVES 4

This recipe for fish stew comes from Bari, an ancient city on the Southern Adriatic coast. If Paris had the sea, it would be a little Bari, so say the natives.

INGREDIENTS

1/2 cup olive oil	Salt and pepper to taste
2 garlic cloves, minced	5 to 7 ounces black olives (preferably small ones)
1 pound, 10 ounces fresh (or 1 1/2 pounds canned) tomatoes, peeled and chopped	4 large thin steaks of grouper, or any other large fish
2 tablespoons chopped fresh parsley	

METHOD

■ Heat the olive oil in a wide, low-sided, flameproof dish (the Italian dish of this sort is called a *teglia*). Add the garlic and sauté for a few minutes. As soon as the oil begins to "sing," add the tomatoes, the parsley, and salt and pepper. Cook for a few minutes over medium heat; then add the olives. Add the fish steaks and cook until they turn fully white 5 to 10 minutes, no longer. Serve hot.

Zuppa alla Contadina

ITALIAN COUNTRY SOUP

SERVES 4

INGREDIENTS

1/4 cup olive oil	2 tablespoons tomato paste
1 small onion, chopped	Pinch chopped fresh parsley
1 garlic clove, minced	1 teaspoon salt
2 celery ribs with leaves, chopped	1/2 teaspoon black pepper
1 small carrot, chopped	1 quart chicken or beef stock
1 potato, peeled and chopped	Grated Parmesan cheese
1 tomato, chopped	Extra-virgin olive oil

METHOD

■ Heat the olive oil in a stockpot. Add the vegetables; stir in the tomato paste, parsley, salt, and pepper. Sauté until the vegetables are softened. Add the broth and heat until the soup begins to boil. Ladle the hot soup into individual bowls. Sprinkle with Parmesan cheese, then olive oil, and serve.

Minestra Di Lenticche

LENTIL SOUP

SERVES 4

Lentils are popular throughout Italy. In some areas, they are served on New Year's day to bring wealth in the coming year.

The greenish-brown Italian lentils tend to retain their shape better than the common variety. If you can find them, use them for this recipe.

INGREDIENTS

1/2 pound (or slightly less) green lentils	3 celery ribs, chopped
1 bay leaf	1 medium-size onion, chopped
2 leaves fresh sage or 1/8 teaspoon dried	2 tablespoons tomato paste
2 tablespoons oil	Salt and pepper to taste
3 slices bacon, julienned	1/4 pound uncooked ditalini
1 garlic clove, minced	Grated Parmesan cheese (optional)

METHOD

■ Simmer the lentils in 3 quarts water with the bay leaf and sage. Do not allow the water to boil too rapidly or the lentils will break.

■ Meanwhile, heat the oil in a large saucepan, add the bacon, and cook until limp. Add the garlic, celery, and onion, and continue to sauté slowly. Dilute the tomato paste in 1/2 cup hot water, and add to the saucepan. Add the salt and pepper. Cook for 20 minutes.

■ When the lentils are tender, add them to the large saucepan. Taste for salt, and add water if the soup is too thick. Bring the soup to a boil again; add the pasta. Cook for 10 more minutes. Remove the bay leaf and sage. Serve with grated Parmesan, if desired.

Zuppa di Fagioli

BEAN SOUP

SERVES 4

Spinach beet (*barbatietola*) is a beet grown for its greens; its root is not eaten. Other greens can be substituted.

INGREDIENTS

1 pound dry small white beans	1 1/2 pounds Swiss chard, spinach beet, or beet greens, finely chopped
3 tablespoons olive oil	Salt and pepper to taste
1 red onion, finely chopped	1 beef bouillon cube
2 small carrots, finely chopped	4 slices hard, stale bread
2 celery ribs, finely chopped	1/2 red onion or 1 scallion, chopped
1 tablespoon tomato purée	

METHOD

■ Soak the beans overnight in water to cover. Drain and rinse. Place in a pot with plenty of water and simmer until soft, 1 to 2 hours.

■ Heat the oil in a saucepan. Add the onion, carrots, and celery and sauté for 10 minutes. Add the tomato purée, greens, salt and pepper, and bouillon cube; simmer for 15 minutes. Add the beans with the cooking water and simmer for 1 hour, adding more water if the soup gets too thick.

■ Place the bread in individual bowls. Pour the soup over the bread, and let sit for 5 minutes. Sprinkle the red onion over the soup and serve.

Passato di Patate con Aglio Arrosto

CREAM OF POTATO SOUP WITH ROASTED GARLIC

SERVES
4 TO 6

In the land of pasta and rice, potatoes have never become commonplace as they have in the rest of Europe, even though they have been cultivated in Italy since the late 1500s. Potatoes are found mainly in the North, where they are often made into gnocchi. Here they are combined with roasted garlic to make an exquisite soup with a mellow garlic flavor.

INGREDIENTS

4 whole garlic bulbs	2 cups homemade chicken stock
Virgin olive oil	2 cups whipping cream
1/4 pound unsalted butter	1 sprig fresh thyme, minced
2 leeks, chopped	Salt and pepper to taste
10 large new red potatoes, peeled and cut into chunks	

METHOD

■ Slice the top off of each head of garlic so that each clove is exposed. Place exposed side up in a shallow baking pan. Drizzle liberally with olive oil. Cover the pan with foil and bake at 275° F for 2 hours.

■ Place the butter and leeks in a heavy 2-quart saucepan. Sauté over low heat for 10 minutes. Add the potatoes and cook, stirring occasionally, for 15 minutes. Add the chicken stock, cover, and simmer until the vegetables are very tender.

■ Squeeze the roasted garlic cloves into the saucepan. Purée the contents of the pan in a food processor or blender to a very smooth consistency. Return the soup to the pan, and add the cream, thyme, and salt and pepper. Serve hot.

Italian Wedding Soup

SERVES 12

INGREDIENTS

MEATBALLS

1/2 pound lean ground beef

1/4 cup chopped fresh parsley

1 1/2 teaspoons salt

1 1/2 teaspoons black pepper

1/2 cup grated Parmesan cheese

2 eggs

SOUP

3 tablespoons clarified butter or olive oil

1 1/2 cups diced onion

1 1/2 cups diced celery

1 1/4 cups diced carrots

1 bunch fresh escarole, chopped

1 small bunch fresh chicory, trimmed

1 bay leaf

Salt and pepper to taste

8 cups chicken broth

1 pound boneless chicken breast

4 ounces uncooked thin egg noodles

1/4 cup grated Parmesan cheese

METHOD

■ Combine the meatball ingredients in a bowl; mix them well by hand. Set aside.

■ Heat the clarified butter in a large soup kettle. Add the vegetables, and sauté for 10 to 15 minutes, or until they are half-cooked. Add the bay leaf and salt and pepper. Pour in the chicken broth. Simmer for about 1 hour.

■ While the soup simmers, steam or bake the chicken breast until done, 35 to 40 minutes. Cool, then slice it into strips. Roll the ground beef mixture into 3/4-inch balls. Add the meatballs and the chicken strips to the soup. Simmer for 10 minutes.

■ Meanwhile cook the egg noodles according to the package directions. Drain and noodles and add them to the soup. Stir in the remaining 1/4 cup Parmesan cheese and serve.

PASTA & SAUCES

▲▲▲▲▲▲▲▲▲▲▲▲▲▲▲▲▲

The book *De Onesta Voluptate*, written in the Middle Ages, honors Signor Meluzza of Como (near Milan) as the inventor of spaghetti (he prepared his with oil and garlic). The *Onesta Voluptate* is on display at the Museum of Pasta in Pontedassio, on the Ligurian Sea, along with other books and drawings that "prove" that pasta originated in northern Italy.

Actually the debate still rages over whether the Italians or the Chinese invented pasta. My opinion is that while China long ago introduced rice-flour noodles, the Italians were first to make semolina wheat pasta—what we traditionally think of as pasta. Actually, the ancient Greeks and the Etruscans both left evidence that they made some sort of noodle, well before the Romans. In any event, by the time of the Renaissance, pasta was widely known, though it remained a luxury food enjoyed by the wealthy and served by the common folk only on special occasions.

Pasta did not become a daily dish in Italy until someone thought of flavoring it with tomatoes, a vegetable native to the Americas. A strain of yellow tomatoes reached Italy in the sixteenth century, but it wasn't until two Jesuit priests brought over from Mexico some seed of the red variety that tomatoes gained a foothold in the cuisine. Of all the Europeans, the Neapolitans were the most enthusiastic about the tomato—and about pasta.

PASTA SHAPES

These shapes are all available in the U.S. Most can be found in Italian markets and specialty food stores, if not at your supermarket.

Agnolatti
"Fat little lambs." Plump, semicircular or square ravioli filled with meat. A holiday favorite of the Piedmont region.

Alphabets
Tiny pasta letters.

Angel Hair (Capelli d'Angeli)
Fine, long, coiled strands of pasta called angel hair because of the fineness, used in soups or with sauces.

Anelli
"Little rings" for soup.

Anellini
Tinier rings.

Anolini
Round or ring-shaped ravioli, served with sauce or in a broth.

Ave Maria
So named because they are shaped like rosary beads. Short tubular pasta for soup.

Bacatilli (or Percateli)
Thin spaghetti with a hole through the middle, used like spaghetti.

Bows (or Farfalle)
"Butterflies" come in small, medium, and large and in colored vegetable flavors. They can be made with eggs or just flour and water.

Cannelloni
A large (usually 4-inch to 6-inch) tubular pasta that can be stuffed with a number of fillings: spinach, ricotta, meat, or a combination. "Large reeds" is the translation. They can be made fresh or are available in dried squares or tubes.

Capellini (or Fideo, Fidelini)
"Fine hairs" to be used in soup or with sauce, often sold coiled; they are not as fine as angel hair.

Capelleti
"Little hats" can be made with fresh dough and stuffed or bought dried and used like macaroni.

Cavatelli
A short, curled noodle formed like a shell.

Conchiglie, Conchigliette (or Maruzze, Maruzelle)
"Conch shells" come in a variety of sizes from tiny shells for soup to giant shells for stuffing. They can be either smooth or ridged.

Creste di Galli
"Cockscombs" can be used in place of medium-size elbow macaroni.

Ditali, Ditalini (or Tubbetti)
"Thimbles" of macaroni cut in short lengths, about 1/4 inch in diameter by 1/2 inch long. Used in soups.

Ditali Rigati
"Ridged thimbles"; they can be sauced, baked, or used in salads.

Elbow Macaroni
Short, curved tubes of pasta, available in many vegetable colors and sizes, from tiny elbows for soups to 1-inch elbows for casseroles.

Farfalle, Farfallette, Farfalloni
(see Bows)

Fettuccine, Fettuccelle

"Little ribbons." A long, flat noodle, about 1/4 inch to 3/8 inch wide. Fettuccine is the Roman version of tagliatelle, most commonly found in yellow or green. Often made fresh, but also available dried, straight or in coils. Fettuccine combines well with most sauces.

Fideo, Fidelini *(see Capellini)*

Fusilli

Long strands of pasta twisted like a corkscrew and used in place of spaghetti. Some manufacturers use the name fusilli for rotelle.

Funghini

Intricate, baby-size "mushrooms" for soup.

Garganelli

Ridged, rolled tubes with diagonal-cut ends. Used in baked pasta dishes.

Gemelli

"Twins." Paired strands of spaghetti about 3 inches long, twisted like embroidery thread. Used like spaghetti.

Gnocchi

Homemade "lumps" that look like dumplings. They can be made with mashed potatoes, cornmeal, ricotta cheese, or semolina. Manufacturers make a dried gnocchi to be used as one would use medium-size elbow macaroni.

Lasagna, Lasagne

Flat, wide sheets of pasta, with straight or curly edges on one or both sides, in yellow or green, for a baked layered meat and cheese dish. Size varies from 1 to 2 1/2 inches wide.

Linguine, Linguini

"Little tongues" are long, thin, flat noodles, halfway between a flat ribbon and a cylindrical strand. Linguine is thinner than fettuccine, wider than spaghetti.

Lumache

"Snails" come in small and medium sizes for salads, baked dishes, and sauced entrées. Use as you would medium elbows.

Macaroni

This is the U.S. pasta industry's generic term for any dried wheat pasta product. More commonly, macaroni means dried pasta tubes.

Maccheroni *(Macaroni)*

Hollow pasta. Elbow macaroni has a slight bend in the middle. Other shapes include bucatini, cannolichi, and ziti.

Maccheroni alla Chitarra

Noodles made on a noodle-cutting instrument that is strung with wires like a guitar, producing long, hollow macaroni.

Mafalde, Mafaldine

Long noodles, about 3/4 inch wide, rippled on both edges (the thinner version being mafaldine). Sauce as for spaghetti or fettuccine.

Maltagliati

Hard-to-find flat noodles with diagonal-cut or pointed ends. Use as you would egg noodles, fettuccine.

Manicotti

"Little muffs" are actually one of the larger tubes of pasta available, ribbed or smooth, for stuffing, saucing, and baking.

Margherita

"Daisy" noodles don't look like daisies. They are about as wide as fettuccine and have one curly edge.

Maruzzel, Maruzze, Maruzelle

A variety of "conch shell" (*conchiglie*) for soups (tiny shells) or stuffing (large shells).

Monti

American ravioli resembling little boats.

Mostaccoli *(or Penne)*

"Mustaches" are 2-inch-long, smooth or ridged, diagonal-cut tubes resembling quill pens (*penne*). They are good with a chunky meat sauce or robust tomato sauce.

Occhi di Lupo

"Wolf's eyes" are thick, elbow-like tubes, 1 1/2 inches long. Good with robust sauces.

Occhi di Pernice

Little "partridge eyes" for soup.

Orzo

"Barley" for soup, sometimes cooked like rice.

Pansotti

"Potbellied" triangular ravioli. These are popular around Genoa.

Pappardelle

A thin, lasagne-like noodle, 1 inch wide, often homemade with pinked edges. These are served with rabbit in Tuscany.

Pastina

General term used for tiny pasta meant for soup.

Paternoster Rigati

"Our Father" pasta is named after beads of the rosary; they are small ridged pastina for soup.

Penne, Pennette *(see Mostaccoli)*

Diagonal-cut, plain or ribbed.

Perciatelle, Bucatini

Flat, hollow spaghetti.

Ravioli

Usually square pasta stuffed with eggs, vegetables, meat, or cheese and served with sauce or in soup. Other (smaller) ravioli are called anolotti or raviolini.

Ricci, Riccini

"Little curls" about 1 1/2 inches long. Use as you would use medium-size macaroni.

Rigatoni

Large ribbed tubes, good with chunky sauces. About 1 1/2 to 3 inches long.

Rotelle

"Little wheels" that are actually corkscrew or spiral shaped. Sometimes also called fusilli, but wider than fusilli. Use as you would medium-size macaroni.

Ruote

"Wheels" that look like their name. Use as you would medium-sized macaroni.

Semi di Melone

"Melon seeds" pastina.

Spaghetti, Spaghettini, Spaghettoni

"Little strands" are the best-known pasta and can be thick or thin. Other varieties of spaghetti are capellini, fidelini, vermicelli.

Stuffed Pasta *(Ravioli, Cappelleti, Tortellini)*

The stuffing can be fish, chicken, meat, cheese, vegetables, or a combination. They are served with sauce or melted butter.

Tagliatelle, Tagliolette, Tagliolini, Tagliarini

The verb *tagliare* means "to cut" and these are narrow-cut egg noodles, 1/8 inch to 3/4 inch wide. Similar to fettuccine in appearance and use, these are the Bolognese version of fettuccine.

Tonnarelli

Square-cut spaghetti.

Tortiglioni

Wider than rotelle corkscrew but similar in appearance and use.

Tortelli (*see also Capelletti*)

"Little twists" rumored to have been modeled after Venus's navel. A Bolognese specialty, filled like ravioli and served with sauce or in soup. Tortellini have smooth edges rather than ruffled ones as capelletti.

Tripolini

Named to honor Italy's conquest of Tripoli, these 1/2-inch crimped-in-the-middle pastas go in soups or salads or can be served with a simple sauce.

Tufoli (*see Rigatoni*)

Vermicelli

"Little worms." Thicker than angel hair, thinner than spaghetti, sold either in straight rods, or in a bow-knot of 15 or 20 strands, or coiled.

Wheels (*see Ruote*)

Ziti

"Bridegrooms" are tubular macaroni, sometimes sold long, then broken into pieces for cooking. They are thinner than mostaccoli but used similarly.

PASTA POINTERS

If you are not going to serve it right away, fresh pasta can be stored in the refrigerator for about a week or in the freezer for 2 to 3 months. Uncooked dry pasta can be stored for up to 1 year in a cool, dry place.

Most dry pasta doubles in volume when cooked, so when measuring uncooked portions, half of what would seem a single serving is a full serving. Measure uncooked dry pasta by weight rather than volume for recipe accuracy. Generally, a serving of pasta is about 2 ounces of cooked or fresh pasta for a first course or side dish; 3 to 4 ounces for the main course.

Use a large, deep pot and about 4 quarts of water for each pound of pasta (1 quart for every 4 ounces, or 2 main course servings). Bring the water to a rapid boil before adding the pasta for even cooking without sticking. Lasagna noodles may require a tablespoon or two of oil in the water to prevent sticking or tearing.

If the pasta is to be used in a casserole, reduce the boiling time by about one-third. The pasta will soften as the casserole bakes.

Pasta is at its best freshly cooked and hot, but it can be kept fresh in the refrigerator for up to 1 week if it is tossed with a bit of butter to prevent sticking. To reheat, drop into boiling water briefly, drain, and use immediately. A tomato-meat sauce often tastes even better after it has been stored in the refrigerator for a few days. If the sauce is mixed with pasta before refrigerating, replace lost moisture with some water before reheating.

THE SAUCES OF ITALY

Aglio-Olio-Peperoncino—Garlic, olive oil, sweet peppers, anchovies, Parmesan

Agra Dolce—Sweet and sour sauce (Milan)

al Burro—Butter and grated Parmesan

al Peperoncino—Red pepper sauce

al Sugo—Tomato sauce and Parmesan

Amatriciana—Tomatoes, red peppers, bacon, onions, garlic

Besciamella—Cream sauce (northern Italy)

Bolognese—Tomatoes, meat, onions, herbs (Bologna)

Carbonara—Smoked ham (bacon), cheese, eggs, olive oil

Carrettiera—Tuna, mushrooms, tomato purée, ground pepper

con le Vongole—Clams, garlic, parsley, pepper, olive oil, sometimes tomatoes

di Fegatini—Chicken liver sauce

di Formaggio—Cheese sauce

di Funghi—Mushroom sauce (from Verona)

di Noci—Walnut sauce from northern Italy

di Pomodoro—Tomato sauce

di Zucchini—Zucchini sauce (from Marches)

Grano en Indiano—Curried corn sauce

Marinara—Tomatoes, olives, garlic

Pizzaiola—Thick, tomato sauce with garlic

Pesto—Basil leaves, garlic, cheese, sometimes pine nuts and marjoram (from Genoa)

Pommarola—Tomatoes, garlic, basil

Puttanesca—Capers, black olives, parsley, garlic, olive oil, black pepper

Ragu—Same as Bolognese

Verde—Parsley, basil, pine nuts

Pasta all'Uovo

EGG PASTA

SERVES 3 TO 4 (ABOUT 1 POUND)

Many of the restaurants I visited made their own pasta and included a recipe for making pasta along with the sauce recipes I collected. The recipes all call for flour, eggs, and salt. The exact proportions of these ingredients vary significantly, but that has more to do with the type and freshness of flour, the prevailing climate, and the size of the eggs than anything else. The very general rule of thumb is to use 1 medium-size egg to 3/4 cup flour.

What follows is a recipe for making Pasta All'uovo (egg pasta) that works whether you make it the traditional Italian way, mixing the ingredients by hand, or whether you use a food processor.

INGREDIENTS

2 1/4 cup all-purpose unbleached flour	1/4 teaspoon salt
3 eggs	

METHOD

■ Pour the flour onto a smooth working surface and gather it into a mound. Make a well in the center.

■ Beat the eggs with the salt and pour into the center of the flour. Start beating the eggs with a fork. With your free hand, push the flour up around the eggs to keep the eggs from spilling onto the table. When the dough can no longer be worked with a fork, knead in the remaining flour with your hands. Continue to knead the dough until it is smooth and elastic and all the flour is worked in. If the dough feels too sticky, add 1 tablespoon of flour at a time and knead it in. If the dough is too dry, add a little beaten egg or oil, a drop at a time.

■ It helps to allow the dough to rest for about 30 minutes before rolling it out, but is not necessary.

■ To make the dough in a food processor, place the flour in the bowl of the machine. Mix in the salt. With the motor running, add the eggs, one at a time. Process until the dough forms into a ball. If the dough seems too sticky, add 1 tablespoon of flour and process for an additional minute. Allow the dough to rest for about 15 minutes before rolling.

METHOD

■ To roll by hand, divide the dough into 4 pieces. Wrap 3 of the pieces in plastic film to keep them moist. Lightly flour the working surface and rolling pin. Flatten the dough into a pancake. Begin to roll from the center out, until you have a sheet of dough the desired thickness, 1/8 inch to 1/16 inch thick (the thickness of a dime). Let the dough rest for about 15 minutes before cutting into the desired shape.

■ To use a pasta roller, divide the dough into 4 pieces. Flatten each piece into a pancake and lightly flour. Wrap 3 of the pieces in plastic film to keep them moist. Set the roller on its widest setting and pull the piece of flattened dough through. Run the dough through the roller again and again, reducing the space between the rollers until the pasta has reached the desired thickness. Let the dough rest for about 15 minutes before cutting into the desired shape.

Note: A recipe for ravioli dough may be found on page 19. A recipe for green lasagna dough may be found on page 68.

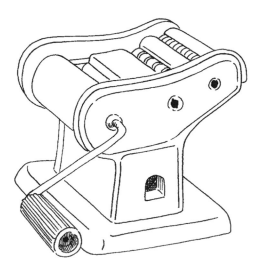

Marinara Sauce

SERVES 6 TO 8

INGREDIENTS

3 tablespoons olive oil

1 onion, minced

1 carrot, minced

1 celery rib, minced

3 garlic cloves, minced

6 fresh basil leaves, minced

1/4 cup minced fresh parsley

6 cups (6 pounds) peeled plum tomatoes, fresh or canned, chopped

Salt to taste

Sugar (optional)

METHOD

■ In a large saucepan, heat the oil. Add the onion, carrot, celery, garlic, basil, and parsley and sauté until the onion is limp, about 5 minutes. Add the tomatoes and salt, stir well, and cover. Bring to a boil, then reduce the heat and simmer for 30 minutes. Taste and adjust the seasonings. The sauce may need a pinch of sugar.

Pasta Aglio Olio

SIMPLE GARLIC SAUCE

SERVES 4

INGREDIENTS

8 to 10 garlic cloves, finely chopped	Fresh Italian parsley
4 tablespoons olive oil	Grated Parmesan cheese
Fresh ground pepper to taste	

METHOD

- Sauté the chopped garlic in the olive oil. Be careful not to brown the garlic.

- Toss with 1 pound of cooked linguini or angel hair pasta. Add salt and freshly ground black pepper to your taste.

- Before serving, you can add a handful of chopped Italian parsley. Toss quickly and serve. Pass grated Parmesan cheese at the table.

Tomato Garlic Sauce

SERVES 4

This sauce is Sicilian. Simple and simply delicious. It is not cooked.

INGREDIENTS

12 plum tomatoes, peeled and finely crushed	1 cup grated Romano cheese
12 garlic cloves, minced	Salt and pepper to taste
1 cup olive oil	Fresh basil leaves

METHOD

- Mix the tomatoes, garlic, and oil in a bowl. Add the grated cheese, salt and pepper. This is just the right amount of sauce for 1 pound of pasta. Garnish with basil leaves.

Pesto

SERVES 4

Pesto is a Ligurian specialty. The Genovese serve it with pasta, minestrone, or as a flavoring in vegetable dishes. Traditionally, pesto is made with a mortar and pestle (hence the name), but you can use a food processor or blender if you prefer. Well sealed in a jar with a thin film of olive oil, pesto can be kept for a week or so in the refrigerator. It also freezes well.

INGREDIENTS

PESTO

1/4 cup basil leaves

1 to 2 garlic cloves

2 to 3 tablespoons pine nuts

Pinch salt

1 cup grated Parmesan cheese

1/4 cup olive oil

METHOD

■ Pound the basil in a mortar with the garlic, pine nuts, and salt. Add the cheese and continue to pound until the mixture is reduced to a paste. Incorporate the oil, little by little, until all has been absorbed.

■ Boil the tagliatelle in water and drain. Put it on a heated serving dish. Pour the pesto over the pasta and serve.

Porcini Sauce

MUSHROOM SAUCE

YIELD: ABOUT 2 CUPS

INGREDIENTS

1/4 pound dried porcini mushrooms	4 tablespoons butter
3 sweet Italian sausages	1 tablespoon tomato paste
1 small red onion, finely chopped	2 cups beef broth, divided
1 garlic clove, minced	Salt and pepper to taste
1 cup minced fresh Italian parsley	1 tablespoon all-purpose flour
1/4 cup olive oil	

METHOD

■ Soak the mushrooms in 3 cups of hot water for 1 hour. Drain and save the water for a soup or sauce.

■ Remove the skins from the sausages, break up the meat, and combine with the onion, garlic, and parsley.

■ Heat the oil and 3 tablespoons of the butter over medium heat; then add the pork mixture. Sauté for 5 minutes.

■ Dissolve the tomato paste in 1/2 cup of the broth. Add the pork and cook for 5 minutes. Add the porcini mushrooms and another 1/2 cup of broth. Season with salt and pepper. Reduce the heat and cook for another 30 minutes, adding the remaining 1 cup of broth as needed.

■ Mix the remaining 1 tablespoon of butter with the flour until completely blended. Add to the sauce and stir well. Cook for 5 minutes.

Carbonara Sauce

CHARCOAL MAKER'S STYLE SAUCE

SERVES 4

This is a very popular pasta dish that originated in Rome. Its popularity was spread outside of Italy by Allied soldiers, who perhaps appreciated the dish for its familiar ingredients: the bacon, cheese, and eggs.

The white wine here is used by the chef to cut the fattiness of the bacon.

INGREDIENTS

8 tablespoons olive oil	4 eggs, lightly beaten
8 slices bacon, cut into bite-size pieces	Grated Parmesan cheese
2 tablespoons white wine	

METHOD

■ Heat the oil in a frying pan. Add the bacon and wine and fry the bacon until crisp. With a slotted spoon remove the bacon pieces to paper towels and reserve the drippings.

■ Drain cooked pasta, return it to the empty pot, and immediately add the drippings and raw egg. (The pasta must be very hot when the egg is poured over it so the egg will cook a bit.) Toss for a couple of minutes until the egg begins to thicken. Drain slightly, place the pasta in a serving bowl, and sprinkle with the bacon pieces and Parmesan cheese. This sauce is enough for 1 pound pasta

Ragu all Bolognese

BOLOGNESE MEAT SAUCE

SERVES 6

INGREDIENTS

6 tablespoons butter, divided	1/4 cup sausage meat
2 1/2 tablespoons olive oil	2 to 3 chicken livers (optional)
1 onion, finely chopped	2/3 cup dry white wine
1 carrot, finely chopped	Salt and pepper to taste
1 celery rib, finely chopped	4 teaspoons tomato paste
2/3 cup finely chopped bacon	1 1/4 cups beef broth, divided
3/4 cup minced pork	1/4 cup light cream or milk
3/4 cup minced beef	Sautéed chopped mushrooms (optional)

METHOD

■ Heat 3 tablespoons of the butter and all the oil in a deep frying pan. Add the onion, carrot, celery, and bacon. Fry until the vegetables begin to change color. Add the pork, beef, sausage, and, if desired, livers. Fry, crumbling the meat with a fork, until it begins to brown. Moisten with the wine and cook until the wine evaporates. Season with salt and pepper, then stir in the tomato paste and a little beef broth. Cover and cook slowly, stirring from time to time, gradually adding remaining broth.

■ After the sauce has simmered for 1 1/2 hours, stir in the cream and cook until the sauce is reduced. Add the remaining butter, and stir until the butter is melted and combined with the sauce. (If desired, sautéed chopped mushrooms can be added at this point.)

Ragu al Tartufo

TRUFFLE SAUCE

SERVES 4

While the black truffle is most prized in French cuisine, the white truffle, which can be eaten uncooked, is more prized in Italy. The flavor and aroma of truffles are almost beyond words. Some describe the white truffle's piquant, earthy flavor as a cross between a clove of garlic and a piece of Parmesan. A little shaving of truffle can elevate a simple dish of buttered noodles to heavenly fare.

INGREDIENTS

6 tablespoons butter	1 small truffle (black or white), grated
1/4 cup olive oil	1 tablespoon chopped fresh parsley
1 tablespoon chopped onions	Salt to taste

METHOD

■ In a pan, heat the butter and olive oil together. Add the onions and sauté briefly. Add the grated truffle, parsley, and salt; sauté for few minutes.

■ This sauce should be mixed with hot, drained noodles and cooked for a few minutes. Serve immediately.

Gorgonzola Sauce with Broccoli

SERVES 4

INGREDIENTS

4 tablespoons olive oil	1 cup chicken stock
1 pound boneless breast of chicken, cut in strips	White pepper to taste
1 red bell pepper, julienned	1/4 cup heavy cream
1 cup crumbled Gorgonzola cheese	7 broccoli florets, blanched

METHOD

■ Heat the olive oil in a frying pan. Add the chicken and the red pepper, and sauté them until they are cooked half through. Add the Gorgonzola, chicken stock, white pepper, and cream. Cook until the liquid is thick.

■ Add the blanched broccoli florets. This sauce is about right for 1 pound of pasta. I recommend linguini.

Puttanesca Sauce

SERVES 4

Puttanesca, "in the manner of a whore," is a fragrant, hearty tomato sauce said to have been invented by the prostitutes of Naples to lure prospective customers to their doors. The basic puttanesca should have olive oil, olives, garlic, anchovies, and capers—everything else is optional and to your own taste, "depending on whom you want to seduce."

INGREDIENTS

1/2 cup olive oil

1 small onion, chopped

4 ounces pancetta, finely chopped

1/4 teaspoon salt

1/2 teaspoon ground black pepper

2 teaspoons crushed hot red pepper

Dash cinnamon

1 tablespoon dried basil

1 tablespoon dried oregano

1 tablespoon dried thyme

Pinch dried tarragon

2 garlic cloves, minced

8 cups or 2 (28-ounce) cans peeled Italian plum tomatoes, crushed by hand

1 (12-ounce) can tomato paste

3 tablespoons pesto (see page 42)

3 ounces pine nuts

1 (3-ounce) jar capers, drained

3 ounces (3/4 cup) black olives, pitted and sliced

1 (4 3/4-ounce) jar marinated artichoke hearts, with liquid

6 anchovy fillets

1 tablespoon honey

Grated Parmesan cheese

METHOD

■ Heat the oil in a large saucepan. Add the onion, pancetta, salt, black and red pepper, cinnamon, herbs, and garlic. Sauté until the onion is wilted. Add the remaining ingredients, except the cheese, and simmer very gently for 1 hour. The grated Parmesan cheese can be passed at the table.

Fettuccine Alfredo

SERVES 4

In Italy, you are likely to encounter this very simple dish as *Fettuccine al burro e Parmigiano*, pasta with butter and Parmesan cheese. With cream added it becomes fettuccine all panna, noodles with cream sauce. In the *Classic Italian Cookbook*, Marcella Hazan says Alfredo had a restaurant in Rome, where this dish became famous. She reports he used a gold fork and spoon to give each serving of fettuccine a final toss.

INGREDIENTS

1 pound fettuccine	Freshly ground black pepper
1 pound unsalted butter at room temperature, sliced 1/4 inch thick	Minced fresh parsley to taste
1 pound Parmesan cheese, finely grated	

METHOD

■ Cook the pasta in plenty of boiling water until it is tender but firm. Drain and quickly return the fettuccine to the kettle. Add the butter and cheese, and toss lightly but rapidly until the noodles are evenly coated. Divide the pasta among 4 heated plates. Top with black pepper and parsley.

FETTUCCINE ALFREDO WITH CREAM

Toss hot, drained fettuccine with 1 cup melted butter, 2 cups finely grated Parmesan cheese, and 1 cup warm heavy cream. Top with freshly ground black pepper.

Fettuccine Napoli

SERVES 4

INGREDIENTS

1 pound sausage meat	1/4 teaspoon white pepper
1 pound fettuccine	1/4 teaspoon nutmeg
1 teaspoon butter	1/2 teaspoon salt
1/2 teaspoon minced garlic	1 1/2 cups half-and-half cream
5 ounces fresh broccoli, chopped	1 1/2 cups sour cream
1/2 pound fresh mushrooms, sliced	1 1/2 cups freshly grated Parmesan cheese

METHOD

■ In a large frying pan, brown the sausage meat over medium heat. Drain well on paper towels and crumble. Set aside.

■ Cook the fettuccine in plenty of boiling water until tender but still firm. Drain.

■ While the pasta cooks, sauté the butter and garlic together in a large sauté pan over medium-high heat. Add the broccoli, and sauté for 3 minutes. Add the mushrooms and crumbled sausage. Add the pepper, nutmeg, and salt, and heat until the sausage is warm. Reduce the heat and slowly stir in the half-and-half and sour cream. Add the Parmesan cheese; heat and stir well. When the cheese has melted and the sauce is well combined, add the fettuccine. Mix thoroughly. Serve very hot.

Fettuccine Bolognese

FETTUCCINE WITH MEAT SAUCE

SERVES 2

"This meatiest of the Italian pasta dishes is typical of the northern city of Bologna, where the art of good cooking and good eating is very appreciated," says Italo Carosiello, who provided me with this recipe. "The region is renowned for large farms yielding the best meats in Italy and the factories that preserve those meats as prosciutto (Italian ham), mortadella (Italian bologna), and an array of other goodies."

INGREDIENTS

TOMATO-MEAT SAUCE	FETTUCCINE
1/4 cup olive oil	10 ounces fettuccine, preferably spinach
2 tablespoons minced onion	2 teaspoons butter
1/2 pound lean ground beef	Grated Parmesan cheese
2 tablespoons medium-dry white wine	
3 cups tomato purée	

METHOD

■ Heat the olive oil in a medium-size frying pan. Add the onions and sauté until lightly browned. Add the ground beef, crumbling and stirring it with a fork until it is thoroughly cooked. Then slowly pour in the wine, add the tomato purée, and simmer for 10 to 15 minutes.

■ While the sauce simmers, bring the water for the pasta to a boil, salting it to taste. Cook the fettuccine, stirring lightly, until tender but still firm. Drain well, place in a serving dish, and quickly cover with the sauce. Top with butter and sprinkle with Parmesan cheese.

Fettuccine with Mussels and Broccoli

SERVES 2

INGREDIENTS

24 large mussels, scrubbed and debearded	Salt to taste
10 spears broccoli	1 pinch ground cinnamon
1/2 pound fettuccine	1 cup heavy cream, divided
1 clove garlic minced and mixed with 2 tablespoons butter	2 tablespoons grated Parmesan cheese
	1 teaspoon chopped parsley

METHOD

▪ Steam the mussels until most of the shells open. Drain and shell the mussels; discard any that have not opened.

▪ At the same time, steam the broccoli until just tender; drain.

▪ While the mussels and broccoli cook, boil the fettuccine in plenty of salted water until tender but still firm. Drain. Melt the garlic butter in a frying pan. Add the salt, cinnamon, and 3/4 cup of the cream, and mix thoroughly.

▪ Divide the pasta between 2 plates. Pour the rest of the cream over the pasta, and sprinkle Parmesan cheese and parsley on top. Toss well. Add the mussels and broccoli and toss again. Spoon the cream sauce over all and serve.

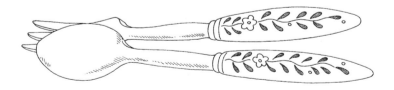

Fettuccine alla Salvia con Funghi Selvatigo

PASTA WITH SAGE, WILD MUSHROOMS, CREAM, AND WALNUTS

SERVES 2 TO 4

INGREDIENTS

4 tablespoons unsalted butter	1/2 pound wild mushrooms (chanterelle, shitaki, oyster, cremini, etc.)
1 cup heavy cream	
1 teaspoon minced garlic	1 tablespoon chopped shallots
1/4 cup chicken stock	1 sprig fresh sage, chopped
Salt and pepper to taste	1/2 pound fresh fettuccine
1 tablespoon olive oil	Toasted walnut, broken in bits

METHOD

■ Melt the butter in a medium-size saucepan and set aside.

■ In a separate saucepan, heat the cream, garlic, and chicken stock; simmer until the liquid is reduced by half. Swirl in the melted butter and season with salt and pepper. Set aside.

■ In the saucepan in which you melted the butter, heat the olive oil. Add the mushrooms and shallots and sauté for 5 minutes. Add the cream sauce and the sage and continue cooking for 2 to 3 minutes.

■ While the sauce cooks, cook the pasta in plenty of boiling water until tender but still firm. Drain. Toss the pasta with the sauce, and adjust the seasonings if necessary. Serve topped with toasted walnuts.

Conchiglioni al Peperoni

SHELL PASTA WITH PEPPERS

SERVES 4

INGREDIENTS

1 pound pasta shells	1 garlic clove, minced
2 green peppers	1 cup minced fresh parsley
6 tablespoons olive oil	2 tablespoons grated Romano cheese
1 1/2 pounds tomatoes, diced	Salt and pepper to taste

METHOD

■ Cook the pasta in plenty of boiling salted water for about 5 minutes. Drain and set aside.

■ Blanch the peppers in boiling water to cover for 2 minutes. Rinse under cold water. Core and secd them; then cut into strips.

■ Heat the olive oil in a large sauté pan. Sauté the pepper strips in the hot olive oil under tender, about 3 minutes. Remove them with a slotted spoon, and set aside. Add the tomatoes to the oil with the garlic and parsley. Simmer for 5 minutes; then add the peppers. Stir in the pasta and mix it with the sauce. Stir in the grated cheese, season with salt and pepper, and serve at once.

Chicken Tetrazzini

SERVES 6

People have eaten an unfortunate number of tetrazzini dishes, made from leftovers and served with other institutional fare, but the original dish is quite tasty. According to legend, this famous pasta dish was named for the Italian coloratura soprano Luisa Tetrazzini, and it is worthy of an aria.

INGREDIENTS

CHICKEN AND STOCK

5-pound to 6-pound stewing hen, with giblets

1 1/2 teaspoons salt

1 small yellow onion

1 medium-size carrot

1 celery stalk

1 bay leaf

3 to 4 peppercorns

1 pound spaghettini or linguine

SAUCE

1/2 cup butter, divided

1/2 pound mushrooms, sliced

1/4 cup flour, sifted

2 cups reserved chicken stock

1 1/2 cups milk, or 3/4 cup each milk and dry white wine

1 cup heavy cream

2 teaspoons salt

1/8 teaspoon white pepper

1 to 2 tablespoons lemon juice (optional)

1/8 teaspoon nutmeg (optional)

TOPPING

3/4 cup fresh bread crumbs

3/4 cup grated Parmesan cheese

METHOD

■ Remove the fat from the body cavity of the hen. Then combine the hen, giblets, salt, onion, carrot, celery, bay leaf, and peppercorns with 1 quart of water in a large heavy kettle. Cover, bring to a boil, and reduce to a simmer. Remove the chicken liver after 10 to 15 minutes; cool and reserve it. Simmer the hen for a total of about 2 hours, until tender. Cool the hen in the stock, then skin the meat and remove the bones. Cut the meat into bite-size chunks and dice all the giblets, including the liver. Skim the stock of fat, strain, and reserve it.

■ Preheat the oven to 350° F.

■ Cook the pasta in plenty of boiling water until tender but still firm.

METHOD

■ While the pasta is cooking, make the sauce. Melt 1/4 cup of the butter in a heavy pan over moderate heat. Add the mushrooms and sauté until limp. Add the remaining 1/4 cup butter and heat until melted. Blend in the flour. Add 2 cups chicken stock and the remaining sauce ingredients and heat, stirring, until thickened. Remove from the heat and keep warm.

■ When the pasta is cooked al dente, drain it and combine it with the sauce and chicken. Place in a buttered, shallow, 3-quart casserole. Mix together the bread crumbs and Parmesan cheese, and sprinkle the topping over the chicken and pasta.

■ Bake, uncovered, for 30 to 40 minutes, until bubbly. Brown quickly under a broiler and serve.

Maccheroni Arrabbiate

ANGRY MACARONI

SERVES 6

Here's a version of an "angry" (spicy) pasta dish from Pisa.

INGREDIENTS

3 pounds tomatoes, peeled	3 garlic cloves
3 tablespoons olive oil, divided	4 small dry red chiles
1/2 pound (2 sticks) butter, cut into pieces	1 pound macaroni
Salt and pepper to taste	Grated Pecorino or other hard cheese

METHOD

■ While the water heats for the pasta, combine the tomatoes, 2 tablespoons of the olive oil, the butter, and salt and pepper in a saucepan. Bring to a simmer, stirring occasionally.

■ Grind the garlic and chiles with 1 tablespoon olive oil in a blender or food processor. Add to the sauce.

■ Cook the macaroni and drain. Add the pasta to the sauce; heat and mix briefly. Serve with grated cheese.

Cavatelli con Rapini

SHELLS WITH RAPINI

SERVES 6

Cavatelli is a short, curled noodle, shaped like a shell. Rapini, or broccoli di rapa, is a pungent, somewhat bitter, nonheading Italian spring green, a leafy broccoli that can be prepared and cooked like spinach.

INGREDIENTS

1 pound rapini (or broccoli)	4 tablespoons butter, cut into small pieces
1 1/2 pounds canned whole Italian tomatoes with basil	Salt and pepper to taste
1 pound pasta shells, cooked and drained	1 cup grated Parmesan cheese

METHOD

■ Place the rapini in a saucepan with salted water. Boil until tender. Drain and keep warm.

■ Crush the tomatoes with your hands. In a saucepan, heat the tomatoes and the basil leaves with which they are canned to a simmer.

■ Add the rapini or broccoli to the tomatoes. Add the butter and salt and pepper. Pour the sauce over the cooked and drained pasta and serve hot. Pass the Parmesan at the table.

Pappardelle all'Ortolana

PAPPARDELLE FARMER'S STYLE

SERVES 4

Pappardelle is a type of homemade noodles. They are usually about 3/4 inch wide and cut with a fluted pastry wheel.

INGREDIENTS

6 artichokes, cleaned	1 pound pasta, preferably pappardelle or fettuccine
About 2 tablespoons olive oil, divided	1/2 pint light or heavy cream
2 cups fresh asparagus tips	2 tablespoons butter
2 cups sliced fresh mushrooms	4 ounces cooked ham, cut into cubes
1 cup fresh peas	Grated Parmesan cheese
1/2 onion	

METHOD

■ Place the artichokes in a deep pan with about 1 1/2 inches of water and a teaspoon of olive oil; cover and simmer for about 30 minutes, or until the artichokes are tender (check with a fork). Cut the artichokes into small pieces, and set aside.

■ While the artichokes cook, prepare the other vegetables. Boil the asparagus tips in salted water for 5 minutes; drain, and set aside. Heat 1 tablespoon of the olive oil in a skillet, add the mushrooms, and sauté for 10 minutes (add a bit more oil if the mushrooms begin to stick); set the mushrooms aside.

■ Boil the peas in salted water with half an onion and a bit of olive oil. Discard the onion and reserve the drained peas.

■ Cook the pasta in plenty of boiling water until tender but still firm. Drain.

■ While the pasta is cooking, make the sauce. In a large skillet, heat the cream and butter. When the butter is melted, add the ham. Heat briefly and then add all the vegetables. Heat for about 5 minutes, stirring occasionally, until all the ingredients are heated through.

■ Toss the pasta into the skillet with the sauce. If the noodles stick together, pour in a little more cream. Add a bit of grated Parmesan cheese. Toss until the vegetables are uniformly distributed, and serve hot.

Rigatoni con Salsicce

RIGATONI WITH ITALIAN SAUSAGE

SERVES 2 TO 3

INGREDIENTS

3/4 pound hot Italian sausages	1 tablespoon chopped fresh oregano
1/4 cup olive oil	1/8 cup finely julienned sun-dried tomatoes
1 green pepper, julienned	
3 garlic cloves, minced	Salt and pepper to taste
Leaves of 1 bunch basil, cut in slender ribbons	1 pound rigatoni

METHOD

■ Preheat the oven to 350° F. Place the sausages in a shallow baking pan. Pierce each twice with a fork. Bake for 25 minutes. Remove the sausages from the pan and slice into 1/8-inch rounds.

■ Begin heating water for the pasta.

■ Heat the olive oil in a large frying pan. Add the pepper and sauté for a few minutes over medium-low heat. Add the garlic and sausages and cook for 10 minutes over moderate heat. Add the basil, oregano, sun-dried tomatoes, and salt and pepper. Remove the pan from the heat and keep warm.

■ When the pasta cooking water comes to a full boil, add the rigatoni. Cook until tender but still firm, then drain the pasta and toss with the sauce. Taste for salt, and serve steaming hot.

Pasta Primavera

PASTA WITH SPRING VEGETABLES

SERVES 4

INGREDIENTS

1 pound pasta (mostaccoli or rigatoni)	2 cups sliced fresh mushrooms
1 tablespoon olive oil	1 cup fresh basil leaves
2 garlic cloves, minced	2 cups chopped broccoli
4 cups diced zucchini	2 tomatoes, diced
1 cup chicken broth	

METHOD

■ While the pasta is cooking, heat the olive oil in a large saucepan. Add the garlic and sauté until golden brown, then add the zucchini and chicken broth. Cook the zucchini briefly, until it is tender but still crisp. Add the mushrooms, basil, and broccoli. Cook until the vegetables are done. When the pasta is tender, but firm, drain and place it in a large serving bowl. Add the vegetables, and toss gently. Garnish with the diced tomatoes.

Tagliatelle al Cucciolo

SERVES 10

Naples is known for its pizza, but that doesn't mean other wonderful dishes can't be had there. This original pasta dish, rich with butter, bacon, cheese, and fresh vegetables, was served to me in a restaurant by the name of al Cucciolo, "the puppy." Why this name was chosen I couldn't say.

INGREDIENTS

1 tablespoon olive oil	2/3 pound Parmesan cheese, grated
3 cups chopped onions	1/2 pound (2 sticks) butter, cut into small pieces
2/3 pound pancetta, cut into strips	
1 pound vine-ripened tomatoes, chopped	5 egg yolks
1 cup fresh or frozen peas	Pinch nutmeg
2 cups hot chicken stock	2 cups cream
2 pounds tagliatelle	1/2 pound mozzarella cheese, sliced

METHOD

▪ In a large ovenproof pan, heat the olive oil. Add the onions and sauté them until the onions are browned, 10 to 15 minutes. Add the pancetta and the tomatoes; sauté for 10 minutes. Then add the peas and the chicken stock and simmer gently.

▪ Cook the tagliatelle in boiling salted water until tender but still firm. When done, fold the noodles into the sauce and sprinkle with the Parmesan cheese. Mix well, then fold in the butter.

▪ Beat the egg yolks with the nutmeg and cream. Fold this mixture into the tagliatelle. Lay the mozzarella slices over the noodles. Bake in a 450° F oven about 10 minutes. Serve hot.

Maccheroni alla Calbrese

MACARONI, CALABRIA STYLE

SERVES 6

Here's another spicy pasta dish, this one with the added richness of Parma ham. The recipe calls for caciocavallo cheese, a piquant cheese made throughout southern Italy. Its name translates as "horse cheese," because it is hung in pairs astride a pole to age and dry. If you like, substitute Parmesan cheese for caciocavallo.

INGREDIENTS

2 1/2 pounds tomatoes	1/4 pound prosciutto (Parma ham), finely chopped
1/2 cup olive oil	
1 garlic clove	Salt and pepper to taste
Small piece hot red chile, finely chopped	5 cups macaroni
1 onion, finely chopped	1 cup grated caciocavallo cheese

METHOD

■ Dip the tomatoes in hot water; then peel them. Halve the tomatoes and discard the seeds. Chop the tomatoes and set aside.

■ Heat the oil in a large pan, add the garlic and chile pepper and sauté briefly. Discard the garlic as soon as it browns. Add the onion, and cook until translucent. Add the ham and continue to cook for 2 to 3 minutes. Add the tomatoes. Season with salt and pepper, increase the heat, and cook briskly for 30 minutes.

■ Bring a large kettle of salted water to a boil, and cook the macaroni until tender but firm. Drain the pasta, return it to the kettle, and toss it with a little of the sauce. Spread a layer of macaroni in a hot serving dish, sprinkle with plenty of grated cheese, and spread over about 2 tablespoons sauce. Continue layering the ingredients until they are all used up. Serve very hot.

Penne al Peperoni

PENNE WITH PEPPERS

SERVES 6

While traveling in Florence, I made the acquaintance of a teacher of Italian cuisine, who shared with me this recipe. It's a first course of pasta seasoned with a 3-colored pepper purée and cream. The dish is very popular with the students at the cooking school.

INGREDIENTS

SAUCE

1/2 cup olive oil

1 medium-size green bell pepper, julienned

1 medium-size red bell pepper, julienned

2 medium-size yellow bell peppers, julienned

1 teaspoon salt

1/2 red onion, finely chopped

2/3 cup light cream

1/2 teaspoon dried oregano

5 tablespoons finely chopped fresh parsley

Freshly ground black pepper

PASTA

1 pound, 5 ounces penne or ridged mostaccoli

3 tablespoons salt

METHOD

▪ Heat the olive oil in a large frying pan over a medium to low flame. Add the peppers, along with the salt and onion, and gently sauté until the peppers are tender, 15 to 20 minutes. With a slotted spoon to drain off excess oil, place the peppers and onion in a blender or food processor, add the cream, and blend on high speed until the sauce is completely smooth. Set aside.

▪ To cook the pasta, add the 3 tablespoons salt to 7 to 8 quarts of water and bring to a boil in a very large (10 quart) covered pot. Add the pasta, separating the pieces immediately with a wooden spoon.

▪ While the pasta is boiling, drain the frying pan of oil and reheat the cream-pepper sauce in it. Add the oregano and chopped parsley.

▪ When the pasta is done, drain it, reserving at least 1/2 cup of the cooking water. Place the pasta in a serving bowl, add the sauce and the cooking water, and toss gently to mix thoroughly. Serve the pasta hot, sprinkled with freshly ground black pepper.

Pennette Arrabbiate

ANGRY PENNETTE

SERVES 4

This is another "angry" pasta. It is hot, pleasantly hot from red chile peppers. It's a quick dish to make; you can prepare the sauce while the pasta is cooking.

INGREDIENTS

4 teaspoons olive oil

2 garlic cloves, minced

1 small dry red chile, finely chopped

1/4 cup finely chopped fresh parsley, divided

3 1/2 cups chopped fresh or canned tomatoes, with juice

Salt and pepper to taste

1 pound pennette rigate (short "ribbed" tubes)

METHOD

▪ While the water heats for the pasta, heat the olive oil in a large saucepan. Add the garlic and chile and fry gently until the garlic is golden. Add half the parsley, and fry for a few seconds until it is "toasted" but not burned. Immediately add the tomatoes and salt and pepper. Stirring occasionally, heat the sauce gently until the pasta is ready.

▪ In the meantime, cook the pasta in plenty of boiling salted water for 8 to 10 minutes, until not quite tender. Drain the pasta well, and add it to the sauce in the pan. Over low heat, mix the pasta and sauce until any excess liquid is absorbed. Serve sprinkled with the rest of the fresh parsley.

Spaghetti, Sicilian Style

SERVES 6

Eggplant and tomatoes are both characteristic of Sicilian cooking

INGREDIENTS

1 large eggplant	Salt and pepper to taste
3/4 cup olive oil, divided	1 teaspoon finely chopped fresh basil leaves or 1 teaspoon dried
2 garlic cloves, peeled and flattened with the side of a knife	1 pound spaghetti
8 large tomatoes (about 3 1/2 pounds), chopped	1/2 cup grated Parmesan cheese

METHOD

■ Peel the eggplant and slice it thinly. Arrange the slices in one layer on a large broiler pan and lightly brush the top of each with some of the olive oil. Set the pan under a hot broiler and brown the slices. Turn the slices over, brushing with olive oil, and brown the second side. Keep the slices warm.

■ In a large saucepan, heat the remaining olive oil (about 1/3 cup). Add the garlic cloves and brown, then remove and discard the garlic, leaving the garlic-flavored oil. Add the tomatoes, salt and pepper, and basil, and cook until they are reduced to a thick purée. Keep warm.

■ While the sauce cooks, boil the spaghetti in plenty of salted water until tender but still firm. Drain the spaghetti and place it on a deep serving platter.

■ Toss the sauce with the spaghetti. Sprinkle with half of the Parmesan cheese. Arrange the eggplant slices, overlapping each other over the spaghetti and cheese. Serve hot and pass the remaining Parmesan cheese at the table.

STUFFED PASTAS

▲▲▲▲▲▲▲▲▲▲▲▲▲▲▲▲▲

These pastas are all made with homemade dough and then stuffed with meat or cheese or both. They take more time to prepare than the pastas in the previous chapter, but can be made ahead and held in the refrigerator or freezer.

In Italy, these pastas are served as a first course, before the meat. However, you will be tempted to make a whole meal out of one of these delicious recipes, and why not?

Lasagna Verdi alla Neapoletana

GREEN LASAGNA FROM NAPLES

SERVES 12 TO 15

INGREDIENTS

PASTA

1 egg white

1 tablespoon olive oil

1 tablespoon salt

1 1/2 cups all-purpose flour

3/4 pound fresh spinach leaves, blanched and chopped finely

MARINARA SAUCE

1/2 cup olive oil

4 cups coarsely chopped onions

2 small carrots, chopped (about 1 cup)

8 garlic cloves, minced

1/2 pound pitted black olives

5 cups (35 ounces) peeled Italian tomatoes, canned with liquid

1/2 cup butter

1 tablespoon finely minced fresh parsley

1 1/2 teaspoons dried oregano

2 teaspoons dried basil or 2 tablespoons fresh

1 teaspoon dried thyme

1 bay leaf

Salt and pepper to taste

1 (6-ounce) can tomato paste (optional)

CHEESE LAYER

1 pound Italian provolone cheese, grated

1 pound ricotta cheese

1 pound mozzarella cheese (the kind made from buffalo is best), grated

1/2 pound Parmesan cheese, grated, plus 1/2 cup for the top of the lasagna

METHOD

■ To make the pasta, beat the egg white with the olive oil and salt. Pour the flour onto a smooth work surface and gather it into a mound. Make a well in the center. Pour the egg mixture and the spinach into the well. Beating with a fork, gradually mix the egg and spinach, then combine them with the flour. If necessary, incorporate a few drops of water. Knead thoroughly to make a smooth dough or blend in a food processor. Wrap the dough in a cloth, and let it rest for 15 minutes. Bring a large pot of water to a boil.

■ Roll the dough very thin and cut into strips 4 1/2 inches wide and 10 inches long. Cook the pasta in boiling water, 5 minutes or less, 2 or 3 strips at a time. Remove the strips, plunge them into cold water, rinse them in running water, and gently squeeze out excess water. Lay the strips on a towel to dry.

METHOD

■ To make the sauce, heat the olive oil in a saucepan. Add the onions, carrots, garlic, and olives and sauté until the onions are transparent. Purée the tomatoes in a food mill. Add the puréed tomatoes to the vegetables. Simmer 15 minutes. Set a sieve over a bowl and pour the sauce through; press with the back of a spoon to push the solids through. Return the strained sauce to the pan. Add the butter, herbs, and salt and pepper; simmer for 15 to 20 minutes. Remove the bay leaf. If the sauce is not thick enough, stir in some or all of the tomato paste.

■ Grease a 9-inch by 13-inch pan. Place a layer of lasagna noodles over the bottom. Alternate sauce and the mixed cheeses between layers of noodles until the lasagna is a couple of inches thick. The last layer should be noodles. Sprinkle the top with the remaining Parmesan cheese and bake at 375° F for 25 minutes.

Lasagna alla Neapoletana

LASAGNA, NAPLES-STYLE

SERVES 8 TO 10

INGREDIENTS

1 pound ground beef or veal	1 teaspoon salt
1/2 pound ground mild Italian sausage	1/4 teaspoon ground black pepper
1 cup chopped onion	10 ounces homemade or packaged lasagna noodles
1 cup chopped mushrooms (optional)	
1 garlic clove, minced	2 eggs, beaten
3 cups tomato purée	2 cups ricotta cheese
1/2 cup dry red wine	1/2 cup grated Parmesan cheese, plus a little more for the top of the lasagna
1 bay leaf	
2 teaspoons dried basil	1/4 cup chopped fresh parsley
1 teaspoon dried marjoram	1/2 pound mozzarella cheese, sliced

METHOD

■ Begin heating water for the pasta.

■ In a skillet, cook the meats, onion, mushrooms, and garlic until the meat is brown. Drain off the fat. Stir in the tomato purée, wine, bay leaf, basil, marjoram, salt, and pepper. Bring to a boil, reduce the heat, and simmer, uncovered, for about 10 minutes, or to the desired consistency, stirring occasionally. Discard the bay leaf.

■ Cook the pasta in plenty of boiling salted water just until tender. Drain, rinse in cold water, and drain again.

■ Combine the eggs, ricotta cheese, Parmesan cheese, and parsley.

■ Grease a 9-inch by 13-inch baking dish and arrange some lasagna noodles in a single layer in the bottom. Spread with half the ricotta mixture, and sprinkle with a third of the mozzarella cheese. Cover with another layer of noodles, topped with half the meat sauce. Add another layer of noodles topped with the rest of the ricotta mixture and a third of the mozzarella,

METHOD

then a layer of noodles topped with the rest of the meat and most of the remaining sauce. Finish with a layer of noodles topped with tomato sauce. Cover the pan with foil.

■ Bake at 350° F for 30 minutes. Top with the remaining mozzarella cheese and a sprinkling of Parmesan. Bake for about 15 minutes longer, or until the cheese is melted and bubbly. Let the lasagna stand for 10 minutes, then cut into squares and serve.

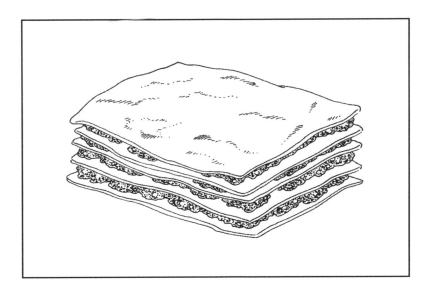

Rollatini alla Valle D'Aosta

ROLLED LASAGNA, VALLE D'AOSTA-STYLE

SERVES 6

From the mountainous region of Italy that borders Switzerland comes this lasagna filled with spiced meat, currants, and pine nuts.

INGREDIENTS

1/2 pound ground, mild Italian sausage	2 cups unsalted chicken or beef stock, divided (preferably homemade)
1 1/2 cups dry red wine, divided	1 tablespoon tomato paste
2 tablespoons olive oil	1/4 cup salted pine nuts
3 medium-size onions, minced	6 tablespoons grated Parmesan cheese, divided
2 1/2 tablespoons minced carrot	
2 bay leaves	1 1/2 tablespoons minced dried currants
1/2 pound lean ground pork	1/2 teaspoon freshly ground black pepper
1/2 pound lean ground beef	1/4 teaspoon salt
2 garlic cloves, minced	12 lasagna noodles (flat, not ruffled)
1/4 teaspoon dried marjoram	1 cup whipping cream
1/8 teaspoon ground cinnamon	Salt and pepper to taste
1/8 teaspoon ground ginger	2 tablespoons shredded fontina cheese
Generous pinch ground cloves	

METHOD

■ In a medium-size heavy skillet, cook the sausage over medium heat until it is well browned on all sides, about 18 minutes. Drain the fat from the skillet, and add 1/2 cup of the wine. Cover and simmer for about 30 minutes. Add a little water to the skillet, if necessary, to prevent sticking. With a slotted spoon, transfer the sausage to a small bowl; crumble when cool. Boil the liquid in the skillet until it is reduced to 1 tablespoon; then pour it over the sausage.

■ Heat the oil in a large heavy skillet over medium heat. Add the onions, carrot, and bay leaves. Cook until the onions are golden, stirring occasionally, about 10 minutes. Add the ground pork and beef, and cook until lightly browned, stirring occasionally, about 20 minutes. Add the garlic and cook for 30 seconds. Stir in the remaining 1 cup wine and the marjoram, cinnamon, ginger, and cloves, scraping up any browned bits. Simmer until the wine evaporates, about 5 minutes. Add the sausage mixture, 1 cup of the stock, and the tomato paste. Cover and simmer for 10 minutes. Uncover and cook until almost all moisture is evaporated. Cool to

METHOD room temperature, and remove the bay leaves. Stir in the pine nuts, 4 table-spoons of the Parmesan cheese, and the currants. Add the pepper and salt.

■ Cook the lasagna noodles in plenty of boiling water very briefly, 5 minutes or less. Plunge them into cold water, rinse them in running water, and gently squeeze out excess water. Lay them on a towel to dry.

■ Preheat the oven to 350° F. Butter an 8-inch by 12-inch baking dish. Spread 1/3 cup of the filling in a 1/8-inch-thick layer over a cooked lasagna noodle, leaving a 1-4-inch border on all edges. Starting at one short end, carefully roll up the noodle to enclose the filling. Place the rolled noodle seam-side down in the prepared dish. Repeat with the remaining noodles to fill the dish.

■ Boil the remaining 1 cup stock until reduced to 1/2 cup. Stir in the cream. Season with salt and pepper. Pour the mixture over the noodles. Combine the 2 tablespoons of fontina with the remaining 2 tablespoons Parmesan cheese, and sprinkle over the noodles.

■ Cover the dish with foil, and bake for 20 to 25 minutes. Uncover and continue baking until the cheese is bubbly, about 10 minutes. Let stand for 10 minutes before serving.

Seafood Lasagna

SERVES 6

INGREDIENTS

12 ounces lasagna noodles	2 tablespoons chopped fresh parsley
2 1/2 cups Marinara Sauce (page 41) or red clam sauce	1 pound provolone cheese (or mozzarella), thinly sliced
1 pound scallops	1 pound ricotta cheese
3/4 pound cooked small shrimp	5 to 6 large shrimp, with their tails, cooked (optional)
1/2 pound mushrooms (preferably canned), sliced	1/4 cup grated Parmesan cheese

METHOD

■ Cook the lasagna noodles in plenty of boiling water until tender but still firm, and reserve them in ice water until needed.

■ Heat the sauce gently in a large pan.

■ Gently cook the scallops, a few at a time, by dropping them in boiling water for 2 minutes. Drain.

■ Add the scallops, small shrimp, mushrooms, and parsley to the warm sauce and stir to combine the ingredients. Spread a small amount of the seafood sauce in the bottom of a 9-inch by 13-inch casserole. Arrange about a third of the lasagna noodles over the sauce. Spread a third of the seafood sauce over the lasagna noodles. Top with a third of the provolone and ricotta cheeses. Repeat the layering two more times, garnishing the top of the lasagna with the large shrimp, if desired. Sprinkle Parmesan cheese over. Bake, uncovered, at 350° F for about 30 minutes; then serve.

Homemade Ravioli

SERVES 12

INGREDIENTS

FILLING

1 carrot, chopped

1 celery rib, chopped

1 small onion, chopped

1/2 pound chopped fresh spinach

1 1/2 cups diced cooked chicken breast

1/2 cup chopped fresh parsley

2 garlic cloves, minced

1 teaspoon dried oregano

1 teaspoon dried basil

1/4 teaspoon pepper

1/4 teaspoon (or less) salt

PASTA AND SAUCE

Double recipe Pasta all'Uovo (see page 39)

12 cups Marinara Sauce (see page 41)

Parmesan cheese

METHOD

■ Steam the carrot, celery, onion, and spinach until just tender. Drain well.

■ Process the chicken and steamed vegetables to make a paste. Add the herbs and seasonings and mix well. Chill.

■ Prepare the pasta dough according to the recipe directions. Let is rest for 30 minutes. Roll into a large 1/8-inch thick rectangle on a large, flat, lightly floured surface. (A ravioli rolling pin and the kitchen table work well.) Spread half the dough with thin layer of filling (also about 1/8-inch thick) and bring the unfilled half of the dough over the filled half to cover it. Roll a ravioli rolling pin over it to mark the squares, or use a wooden yardstick. Cut the ravioli apart with a pastry cutter.

■ Boil the ravioli gently in unsalted boiling water for 12 minutes. Drain carefully and serve with hot Marinara Sauce and Parmesan cheese.

Tortelli d'Erbette

PARMESAN TORTELLI WITH GREEN STUFFING

**SERVES
8 TO 10**

These stuffed pastas are often made for special occasions, such as Christmas and New Year's. This recipe, which hails from Parma, is very typical of the tortelli of the region, with its stuffing of spinach or beet greens and its topping of melted butter.

This recipe was written for use with pastry flour. American all-purpose flour can be substituted, but since it is higher in gluten, you will probably need to use less.

INGREDIENTS

PASTA

2 pounds (about 8 cups) pastry or all-
   purpose flour

6 eggs

FILLING

1 pound spinach or beet greens

1 egg

1 pound ricotta cheese

Salt and pepper to taste

Pinch ground nutmeg

TOPPING

Grated Parmesan cheese

Melted butter

METHOD

▪ Pour the flour onto a smooth work surface and gather it into a mound. Make a well in the center. Beat the eggs and pour them into the well. Beating the eggs with a work, gradually combine the eggs and flour. Beat in 1/2 cup water, a little at a time, and knead thoroughly. Shape into a smooth round mass.

▪ Wrap the dough in cloth and let it rest.

▪ Begin heating water to boil the tortellini.

▪ To make the filling, thoroughly wash the spinach or beet greens. In a saucepan, steam the greens until tender in the water that clings to the leaves after washing. Drain; squeeze out excess liquid. Chop the greens fine.

▪ Beat the egg. Combine the egg, chopped greens, ricotta cheese, salt and pepper, and nutmeg. Refrigerate the stuffing mixture while you roll and cut the dough.

METHOD

■ With a rolling pin, roll out the dough into a very thin layer and cut rectangles about 2 to 3 inches long and 1 to 1 1/2 inches wide. Place a spoonful of filling on each rectangle, and fold the rectangle in half. Press the edges firmly together to seal them.

■ When you run out of dough or filling, gently boil the tortellini for about 5 minutes, or until tender but still firm. Serve sprinkled abundantly with Parmesan cheese and melted butter.

Tortelli de Magro

LEAN TORTELLI

SERVES 8

This dish was traditionally served on Fridays or other days of abstinence and the day before Christmas, as it contains no animal fat and is light and easy to digest. (*Giorno di magro* means day of abstinence in Italian.)

If you use all-purpose flour, you may not need as much. For the filling, I substituted ricotta cheese for the buttermilk curd in the original recipe.

INGREDIENTS

PASTA

1 pound (about 4 cups) pastry flour or all-purpose flour

7 eggs

FILLING

1 pound ricotta

3 1/2 ounces chopped frozen spinach

1 egg

5 ounces Parmesan cheese, grated

Pinch nutmeg

Salt

TOPPING

Melted butter

Grated Parmesan cheese

METHOD

▪ Pour the flour onto a smooth work surface and gather it into a mound. Make a well in the center. Beat the eggs and pour them into the well. Beating the eggs with a fork, gradually combine the eggs and a little water. Knead the dough or blend in a food processor. Wrap the dough in a cloth, and leave it in a cool place for about 1 hour.

▪ Steam the spinach. Drain; squeeze out any excess water. Place the ricotta in a bowl and add the spinach. Add the egg, Parmesan cheese, nutmeg, and salt; mix to a smooth paste.

▪ Roll the dough very thin, in strips about 20 inches long by about 4 inches wide. Place a heaping teaspoonful of the filling every 2 inches along the pasta strips. Fold the pasta strips in half lengthwise, and press the edges to seal them firmly. Then cut the strips into lozenge shapes by making diagonal cuts between the mounds of filling.

▪ Cook the tortelli in plenty of boiling salted water for 8 to 10 minutes; drain well. Serve in heated dishes with melted butter and grated Parmesan cheese.

Cheese-Stuffed Cannelloni

SERVES 6

Cannelloni are sometimes made with crepes, as in this recipe, instead of pasta tubes. To save time, you can substitute 3/4 pound of manicotti tubes, cooked according to package instructions.

INGREDIENTS

BATTER

2 eggs, lightly beaten

3/4 cup milk

1/2 teaspoon salt

1 cup sifted all-purpose flour

FILLING

1 pound ricotta cheese

3 tablespoons grated Parmesan cheese

2 tablespoons minced fresh parsley

1 teaspoon salt

1 egg, lightly beaten

TOPPING

3 cups Marinara Sauce (see page 41)

Grated Parmesan cheese

METHOD

■ Preheat the oven to 350° F.

■ For the crepes, beat together the eggs, milk, and salt. While beating slowly, add the flour and continue to beat until the batter is smooth.

■ Grease a griddle and heat it to moderately hot. Drop spoonfuls of batter, 1 tablespoon for each crepe, onto the griddle, and allow the batter to spread into 4-inch-diameter circles. Flip the crepes when they start to brown and their edges begin to dry. Lightly brown the flip sides. Lay them on paper towels, lightest side down, as you cook the rest.

■ Mix together the filling ingredients.

■ Butter a 9-inch by 13-inch baking dish. Spoon about 1 1/2 tablespoons of the filling mixture on the center of each crepe. Then fold the top and bottom of the crepe toward the center, envelope fashion. Arrange the stuffed crepes seam-side down in the baking dish, and top with the heated sauce.

■ Bake, uncovered, for 30 minutes, or until bubbly. Serve hot with grated Parmesan cheese.

Cannelloni Garibaldi

SERVES 6

INGREDIENTS

Dough for Pasta all'Uovo (see page 39)	1/2 cup finely grated Parmesan cheese
1 pound sweet Italian sausages	1 egg, lightly beaten
1 (10-ounce) package frozen chopped spinach	3 cups Marinara Sauce (see page 41)

METHOD

■ Roll the pasta dough very thin, and cut it into rectangles 3 inches by 4 inches. Bring a large pot of water to a boil. Very briefly cook the pasta strips, a few at a time, then rinse them in cold water and lay them on a towel to dry.

■ Preheat the oven to 375° F. Remove the sausage meat from the casings and brown the meat in a large heavy skillet over moderately low heat for 10 to 15 minutes, stirring occasionally and breaking up large clumps with a spoon. With a slotted spoon, transfer the meat to a bowl.

■ Cook the spinach according to the package directions. Drain, pressing out as much water as possible with a spoon. Add the spinach, 1/4 cup Parmesan cheese, and the egg to the sausage; toss well to mix.

■ Butter a shallow 3-quart casserole. Divide the filling evenly among the pasta strips. Starting at one short end, roll up each of the strips, and arrange them seam-side down in a single layer. Spoon the sauce evenly over all and top with the remaining 1/4 cup Parmesan cheese. Bake, uncovered, for about 30 minutes, until the cheese bubbles.

GNOCCHI, RISOTTO & POLENTA

Dumplings, rice, and polenta—dishes that might be served as side dishes in the typical meat-and-starch meal of the United States (if such a typical meal can be said to exist still)—are first courses in Italian cuisine.

Gnocchi (pronounced knee-o-key) is an ancient dish, first made under the name of ravioli. There are references to these simple dumplings in some of the oldest Italian cookbooks. Gnocchi can be made of various ingredients. In Emilia-Romagna you find *gnocchi verde*, made with spinach, eggs, cheeses, and flour. Roman gnocchi are likely to be made with coarsely ground semolina, eggs, and Parmesan. In Venice, look for gnocchi alla Cadorina, made with potatoes and smoked ricotta. Gnocchi zucca is made with pumpkin. By far, though, the most common type of gnocchi is made with potatoes.

The recipes for gnocchi appear simple, but making a good batch of gnocchi takes practice. The trick is to make the mixture stiff enough to be boiled without falling apart, yet light enough to be tender.

Risottos originated in the North, where rice has had a foothold since it was first introduced, probably in the fifteenth century. A risotto is made by slowly adding the cooking liquid to a special variety of rice, spoonfuls at a time, to produce a creamy mixture, yet with each grain remaining first and separate. Of all the risotto dishes, risotto alla Milanese, a golden rice flavored with saffron, is the most famous. For best results, make risotto with arborio rice, as Italians do. This variety of rice, particularly well suited to producing a creamy risotto, is available at most Italian groceries. Uncle Ben's Converted Rice makes a surprisingly acceptable substitute.

Like gnocchi, polenta is a humble dish, a simple porridge made of cornmeal. While many Italians serve polenta plain or with a sauce, Americans most commonly allow the polenta to cool in a shallow baking pan, then they cut it into slices and bake it with a sauce poured over it. Or it can be simply fried in olive oil and minced garlic.

Cheese Gnocchi

SERVES 4

Serve hot as a lunch entrée or as a substitute for potatoes with veal or chicken.

INGREDIENTS

GNOCCHI

1/2 pound ricotta cheese

1/2 cup all-purpose flour, sifted

6 tablespoons grated Parmesan cheese

3 tablespoons butter, melted

1/2 teaspoon salt

Pinch nutmeg

2 eggs, lightly beaten

TOPPING

1/3 cup melted butter

1/3 cup grated Parmesan cheese

METHOD

■ Preheat the oven to 350° F.

■ Stir together all the gnocchi ingredients and spoon the mixture into a pastry bag fitted with a large pastry tube (with an opening of about 1/2 inch).

■ In a large kettle, heat about 5 quarts salted water to boiling, then reduce the heat to a simmer. Squeeze out the gnocchi mixture over the water, cutting with a knife at 1-inch intervals and letting the pieces drop into the water. Simmer, uncovered, for 2 to 3 minutes, until the gnocchi float, then remove them with a slotted spoon and drain them in a colander.

■ Arrange the gnocchi in a single layer in a buttered 1 1/2-quart shallow casserole, drizzle with melted butter, and sprinkle with Parmesan cheese. Bake the gnocchi, uncovered, for 10 minutes, then broil them for about 2 minutes, until they are lightly browned. Serve hot.

Gnocchi di Patate

POTATO DUMPLINGS

SERVES 4

You are likely to encounter this classic in most trattorias in Rome. It is excellent as a side dish with chicken or veal.

INGREDIENTS

3/4 pound russet potatoes, peeled	Salt and pepper to taste
2 cups all-purpose flour	1 to 2 tablespoons chopped fresh parsley
1/4 pound Romano cheese, grated	1 or 2 garlic cloves, minced
4 egg yolks	Tomato, cream, or meat sauce, heated
1 1/2 ounces butter	

METHOD

■ Boil the potatoes for about 25 minutes until tender. Drain and mash them. Mix in the flour, cheese, egg yolks, and butter. Add the salt and pepper, parsley, and garlic. Knead all together until the dough is firm, though sticky.

■ Begin heating a large pot of water.

■ Shape the dough into long cylinders about 1/2 inch in diameter, and cut the rolls into 1/2-inch lengths. Press each one against the tines of a fork so that one side bears an indentation from your finger and the other side bears the mark of the fork. When the water comes to a boil, drop in the gnocchi, stirring carefully. They will rise to the surface when done. Remove them with a slotted spoon and place them on a serving dish. Pour the sauce over them and serve hot.

Gnocchi di Patate Fritti

FRIED POTATO DUMPLINGS

SERVES 4

These are an excellent accompaniment to roast chicken. The drippings from the chicken serve as sauce for the gnocchi.

INGREDIENTS

1 pound potatoes, peeled	6 tablespoons butter
1 egg, slightly beaten	Olive oil

METHOD

- Boil the potatoes until tender. Drain them and mash them well.

- Mix in the egg and butter.

- Begin heating a large pot of water.

- Shape the dough into thumb-size dumplings. When the water comes to a boil, drop in the gnocchi. Let them cook until they rise to the surface, then drain them well.

- Put at least 1/2 inch olive oil in a deep skillet and heat. When the oil is very hot, slip in the gnocchi. Fry them until they are a uniform golden brown. Serve hot.

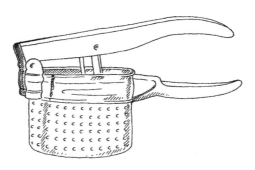

Risotto alla Milanese

SERVES 4

There are dozens of risotti, soft rice mixtures that are to northern Italy what pasta is to southern Italy. This one is a classic, delicious with veal or chicken.

INGREDIENTS

2 tablespoons butter	Pinch powdered saffron, or 1/8 teaspoon saffron threads soaked in 1/4 cup of the hot broth (strain and reserve the broth)
2 tablespoons beef marrow or 1/4 cup butter	
1 small onion, chopped	About 1/2 teaspoon salt
1 cup arborio, short-grain, or Uncle Ben's Converted rice	1/8 teaspoon freshly ground black pepper
	1/4 cup grated Parmesan cheese
2 cups of chicken or beef broth or water, divided	

METHOD

■ Melt the butter or marrow in a heavy saucepan over moderately high heat. Add the onion, and sauté for about 1 minute, until it is a pale golden color. Add the rice and sauté for 1 minute, stirring to coat it with the butter. Reduce the heat to moderate. Add 1/2 cup of the broth, the saffron, salt, and pepper. Cook, stirring constantly, until almost all the liquid is absorbed. While continuing to cook and stir, add the remaining 1 1/2 cups of broth, 1/2 cup at a time. Let the rice absorb the liquid each time before adding more. This will take 30 to 40 minutes. When the risotto is properly cooked, it will be creamy with just the slightest bite. With a fork, lightly mix in the cheese. Taste for salt, and serve.

Risotto con Vongole

RICE WITH CLAMS

**SERVES
4 TO 6**

If you don't have fish stock on hand, you can substitute shrimp stock made from boiling the shells, clam juice, or, even, broth made with fish bouillon cubes.

INGREDIENTS

3 to 3 1/2 pounds small clams in shell	1 cup dry white wine
Salt	Freshly ground black pepper
5 tablespoons olive oil	2 1/2 cubs arborio, short-grain, or Uncle Ben's Converted rice
2 garlic cloves, minced	6 1/2 cups boiling hot fish stock, divided
2 to 3 sprigs parsley, minced	

METHOD

■ Wash the clams thoroughly in plenty of salted water. Heat a heavy frying pan until very hot, add the clams, and shake them over the heat until they open. Cool and shell them.

■ Heat the olive oil in a large pan. Add the garlic and parsley, and sauté until the garlic begins to color. Add the clams, reduce the heat, and simmer for a few minutes. Add the wine and cook until it evaporates; then season generously with pepper. Add the rice, stir gently, and cook until the rice begins to change color. Add a cup of stock and cook over moderate heat until it has been absorbed. Add the remaining 5 cups stock, a cup at a time, until the stock is gone and the rice is tender. Taste for seasoning and serve immediately.

Genoese Rice

SERVES 7

INGREDIENTS

2 cups short-grain white rice	2/3 pound ground veal
2 cups chicken, veal, or beef broth	3 artichokes, trimmed and quartered
2 tablespoons butter	Salt and pepper to taste
1 onion, thickly sliced	Parmesan cheese, grated
Handful chopped fresh parsley	

METHOD

■ Put the rice in a saucepan with a tight-fitting lid. Add the broth, cover, and quickly bring to a boil. Reduce the heat and let the rice simmer.

■ While the rice cooks, melt the butter in a large skillet. Add the onion and parsley, heat until the onions glaze. Add the veal and artichokes.

■ Preheat the oven to 450° F.

■ When the rice has absorbed about half the broth, add it to the veal mixture in the skillet. Cook over a low flame, stirring occasionally. Add a little more hot broth or water, if needed. Add salt and pepper and Parmesan cheese to taste. When the rice is ready (almost dry), pour it into a buttered casserole. Place the casserole, uncovered, in the oven. Remove it when a golden crust forms over the top of the rice. Serve hot.

Suppli

RICE CROQUETTES

SERVES 6

These suppli are Roman egg-shaped rice-balls stuffed with sauce, meat, and mozzarella. In southern Italy and Sicily, similar "rice oranges" are made.

INGREDIENTS

2 cups short-grain white rice	3 egg yolks, lightly beaten
1 teaspoon salt	Handful grated Parmesan cheese
2 1/2 cups Tomato-Meat Sauce (see page 52) or Ragu alla Bolognese (see page 46)	

METHOD

■ Put the rice in a large saucepan with a tight-fitting lid. Add 4 cups water and the salt, cover, and bring quickly to a boil. Reduce the heat and simmer for about 15 minutes, until the rice is tender. Then spread out the rice on a wide plate or serving dish and let it cool.

■ Strain the meat sauce through a sieve onto the rice; reserve the bits of meat and vegetables left in the sieve. Add the egg yolks and Parmesan cheese to the rice and sauce, and mix carefully with your hands until the ingredients are well combined.

■ Heat the oven to 450° F.

■ Take a handful of the rice mixture and form it into a ball. Make a hollow in the middle, stuff the hollow with some of the reserved meat and vegetable bits from the sieved sauce, and seal with some of the rice mixture. Make more balls until all the rice mixture and stuffing is used.

■ Lay the balls on an oiled pan. Bake in the oven until the rice begins to brown. Serve at once.

Polenta con Fagiole

POLENTA WITH BEANS

SERVES 4

My grandmother, Maria Grazia Benevento Dolceacqua, brought this traditional northern Italian cornmeal recipe from Salerno, Italy. It was handed down through four generations from Grandma to late Aunt Philomena and Uncle Frank, to Cousin Anna, and to Anna's children, Tina and Frank Jr.

INGREDIENTS

1 (10-3/4 ounces) can condensed chicken broth	1 cup cooked cannelini beans (or white Italian kidney beans)
1 cup polenta (cornmeal)	Grated Parmesan cheese
8 tablespoons butter, divided	2 cups Marinara sauce (see page 41)

METHOD

■ In a saucepan, bring the broth and 3/4 cup water to a boil. Reduce the heat and simmer.

■ In a bowl, blend 1 cup of water and the polenta until smooth. Pour the polenta mixture into the simmering broth, stirring constantly. Stir in 1 tablespoon of the butter. Add the cannelini beans. Continue stirring over the heat for 20 minutes, or until the polenta comes away from the side of the pan as you stir. Then spoon the polenta mixture into a buttered bowl and let it stand 10 minutes.

■ Unmold the polenta onto a plate, and cut it into thick slices. Serve with the remaining 7 tablespoons butter, melted, and grated Parmesan. If desired, pour marinara sauce over the slices.

SEAFOOD OF ITALY

▲▲▲▲▲▲▲▲▲▲▲▲▲▲▲▲▲

The geography of Italy is such that almost every region has its share of coastline. Seafood ranks just behind pasta in its importance to the Italian diet. The Adriatic Sea and the waters around Sicily are two of the richest fishing regions of the Mediterranean, and the area provides some of the best seafood dishes in Italy.

There are so many Italian recipes for fish that it is difficult to make a selection; there are dozens of fish soups alone. The seven towns of the Marches region all claim the best *brodetto* (fish soup) of that particular stretch of coastline.

If the squid is young, fresh, and properly prepared, it can be exquisite; abused, it can be rubbery and tough. The smaller the squid are, the better.

When cooking squid, plan to serve about 1/3 to 1/2 pound per person. The choicest squid weigh only a few ounces each. For top quality, choose squid that are firm and sweet-smelling with little or no liquid.

If your squid has not already been cleaned at the fish market, lay it on a counter back side up (the back is the side on which the eyes are most fully visible) with tentacles fully extended. With a sharp knife, cut down the center back, exposing the cuttlebone (a transparent bone that looks and feels like plastic). Lift it out and discard it.

Grasp the head and tentacles and pull toward you, turning the squid or octopus inside out and taking care not to rupture the ink sac. Save the sac if you like, and use the ink in broth and stew. Discard all the other internal organs.

Remove the head, eyes, mouth, and parrot-like beak. Cut off the tentacles close to the head, pushing out and discarding the bead of flesh at the root of each tentacle.

Wash the body and tentacles several times in cool water. The squid is now ready for cooking (though you can remove the skin if you want to).

When choosing uncooked clams or mussels for a dish, discard any open or loose-shelled ones. After cooking, discard any mollusks that have failed to open.

When cooking seafood, do not oversalt. Add the salt last, and only to taste. The flavor of most seafood dishes will develop more fully if they are allowed to sit for 15 minutes before serving. Please scrub all shellfish carefully before you use them.

The following recipes for fish and seafood are meant to be used for second-course dishes. To use seafood in antipasto, pasta, and pizza, see the chapters on these subjects.

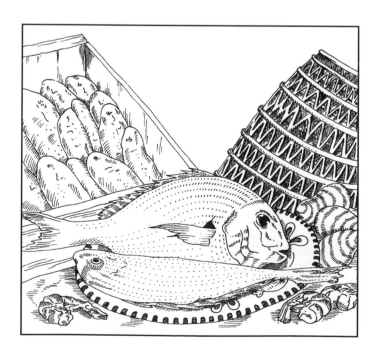

Italian Baked Oysters on the Half-Shell

SERVES 6 TO 8

INGREDIENTS

24 oysters in their shells, thoroughly washed

1 cup fresh bread crumbs

1/3 cup grated Parmesan or Romano cheese

1/4 cup minced fresh parsley

1/2 teaspoon dried thyme

1/8 teaspoon freshly ground black pepper

1/4 cup butter, melted

Rock salt (It retains the heat.)

METHOD

■ Open each oyster and drain. Wash the deep bottom shells. Place each oyster in a bottom shell. Combine the bread crumbs, cheese, parsley, thyme, and pepper. Toss with the melted butter. Spread the rock salt in the bottom of a shallow baking pan. Preheat the oven to 450° F. Top each oyster with about 1 tablespoon of the crumb mixture. Arrange the shells on the bed of rock salt. Bake for 8 to 10 minutes, or until the crumb mixture is lightly browned and the edges of the oysters begin to curl.

Cosmo's Steamed Clams

SERVES 6

INGREDIENTS

2 tablespoons olive oil	1/2 cup butter
2 teaspoons minced garlic	2 teaspoons salt
72 littleneck clams, scrubbed and rinsed	2 teaspoons crushed hot red pepper
5 3/4 cups (46 ounces) clam juice	2 teaspoons dried oregano
1 (15-ounce) can crushed tomatoes	2 teaspoons dried basil
1 cup white wine	2 teaspoons chopped fresh parsley

METHOD

■ In a stockpot or dutch oven, heat the olive oil. Sauté the garlic until golden. Add the remaining ingredients with 2 cups of water. Cover and boil, stirring occasionally. When most of the clams open, remove from the heat, and let stand for 5 minutes. Discard any clams that do not open. Place the clams in soup plates and ladle the broth over.

Mussels Sicilian

SERVES 2

INGREDIENTS

10 mussels, scrubbed and debearded	3 to 4 teaspoons Chablis wine
1 tablespoon olive oil	Salt and pepper to taste
1/4 teaspoon anchovy paste	4 tablespoons Marinara Sauce (see page 41)
1 teaspoon minced garlic	
Pinch ground red pepper	1/4 pound chopped pancetta

METHOD

■ Steam the mussels in a bit of water until they begin to open. Discard any that have not opened. Heat the olive oil in a small saucepan. Add the anchovy paste and garlic with the red pepper and sauté for 40 seconds. Add the Chablis. Combine this mixture with the steamed mussels, stirring it into the liquid in the pot. Fry the pancetta until crisp. Lift out and place on paper towel to drain. Sprinkle over the dish and serve.

Crab Venetian Style

SERVES 5

This exquisitely simple dish can be served as a first course, followed by a green salad dressed with olive oil, salt, and anchovies.

INGREDIENTS

2 pounds crab in the shell	1/4 cup chopped Italian parsley
1/2 cup olive oil	Salt and pepper to taste
1/2 cup sliced leeks	1/2 cup dry white wine
2 garlic cloves, minced	1 tablespoon lemon zest
2 bay leaves	

METHOD

■ Cook the crab in salted boiling water for 20 minutes. Remove it from the pot and let it cool. Remove the crab meat from the shells and cut into cubes. Save the shells for garnish.

■ While the crab is cooking, begin making the sauce. In a medium-size pan, heat the olive oil. Add the leeks and garlic. Sauté until they are light brown, then add the bay leaves, parsley, salt and pepper, and wine. Bring to a boil.

■ Put the crab pieces in a baking dish and pour the boiling sauce over it. Let is rest for about 5 minutes. Sprinkle lemon zest over the crab. Serve with a dry Sardinian white wine, such as Giogantinu di Gallura or Aragosta di Alghero.

Italo's Shrimp Pizzaiola

SERVES 2

Italo created this dish for his wife, who loves seafood. The recipe is typical of the way fish is prepared along the southern coast of Italy.

INGREDIENTS

2 tablespoons olive oil	Salt and pepper to taste
2 tablespoons minced onion	1/8 teaspoon dried oregano
2 tablespoons sliced fresh mushrooms	1/8 teaspoon dried basil
1 medium-size green pepper, chopped	1 small garlic clove, crushed
16 medium shrimp (about 1/2 pound), shelled and deveined	1/4 cup medium-dry white wine
	2 fresh (or canned) tomatoes

METHOD

■ In a skillet, heat the olive oil. Add the onion, mushrooms, and pepper and sauté until they are half-cooked, just beginning to turn color. Add the shrimp, salt and pepper, oregano, basil, and garlic, and sauté for about 5 minutes, until the shrimp are cooked. Slowly add the wine, then the tomatoes, crushing them with a fork and stirring. Simmer until the liquid is reduced by a third. Serve with hot Italian bread.

Antipasti (Appetizers, page 14)

Mussels Sicilian (page 94)

Crab Venetian Style (page 95)

Pollo Ripieno all Lucana (Stuffed Chicken Lucania Style, page 110)

Scallopini al Vermouth (Veal Scallops with Vermouth, page 126)

Ossobuco alla Milanese (Veal Shanks in the Style of Milan, page 127)

Cannoli alla Siciliana (Sicilian pastry tubes, page 175)

Biscotti (Cookies, page 180)

Grandma's Prawns

SERVES 2

INGREDIENTS

1 cup olive oil	1/2 teaspoon crushed hot red pepper
2 garlic cloves, crushed	1/2 teaspoon dried oregano
10 jumbo shrimp, with tail, deveined	10 black olives, pitted
1/4 cup dry white wine	2 medium-size ripe tomatoes, crushed
Salt to taste	2 teaspoons capers

METHOD

■ Sauté the garlic in hot oil until it begins to color. Add the shrimp and cook for about 2 minutes, or until they redden. Add the wine, salt, red pepper, and oregano; stir and cook for another 2 minutes. Add the remaining ingredients, stir, and cover. Reduce the heat and simmer for approximately 6 minutes.

Cerino's Shrimp Sauté

SERVES 4

INGREDIENTS

1 pound (2 cups) clarified butter	1 teaspoon salt
2 pounds shrimp, shelled and deveined	Lemons, quartered
Flour to coat the shrimp	1/4 cup chopped fresh parsley
2 garlic cloves, minced	

METHOD

■ Preheat the oven to 350° F.

■ Put clarified butter on the bottom of a pan. When the butter is hot, add just enough floured shrimp to cover the bottom of the pan. Cook for 1 minute on each side. Add a bit of the minced garlic and salt. Transfer the shrimp to a baking dish and keep warm. Repeat until all the shrimp are done. Squeeze lemon over the shrimp, sprinkle with parsley, and bake for 3 or 4 minutes.

Shrimp Pancettati in Salsa Verde con Risotto

SHRIMP AND ITALIAN BACON IN GREEN SAUCE WITH RICE

SERVES
4 TO 6

The secret to this recipe is using genuine Italian rice. I prefer arborio rice, grown in the Po valley, but any imported Italian variety is fine. In a pinch, Uncle Ben's Converted Rice will do.

INGREDIENTS

SALSA VERDE

1 cup unsalted butter, at room temperature

Leaves of 1 bunch fresh parsley (preferably Italian parsley)

Salt and pepper to taste

1/2 cup whipping cream

RISOTTO

1/2 cup butter

1 cup minced onion

1/4 pound fresh mushrooms, quartered (about 1 cup)

2 cups Italian rice

3 cups chicken stock

Salt and pepper to taste

1/2 cup grated Parmesan cheese

SHRIMP AND PANCETTA

18 jumbo shrimp, shelled and deveined

18 thin slices pancetta

Salt and pepper to taste

About 1/2 cup all-purpose flour

1/4 cup olive oil

METHOD

■ To make the sauce, combine the butter, parsley, and salt and pepper in a food processor, and process until the parsley is finely chopped and the ingredients are well blended. (Or chop the parsley by hand and pound it in a mortar. Gradually work in the butter.) Place the mixture in a bowl and freeze for 10 minutes.

■ While the herb butter chills, make the rice. Melt the butter in a large saucepan over high heat. Sauté the onion and mushrooms for 3 minutes, or until the onions are soft and golden. Stir in the rice and cook for 1 minute. Add the chicken stock, 1 cup at a time. Bring to a boil and simmer uncovered, stirring, for 15 minutes, or until the rice is soft and the liquid is completely absorbed. Add salt and pepper. Press a piece of buttered foil over the rice to keep it warm until you are ready to use it.

■ When the herb butter has chilled, bring 1/2 cup whipping cream to a boil in a shallow pan. Gradually whisk in the herb butter until the sauce is creamy and foamy. Keep the sauce warm.

METHOD

■ Preheat the oven to 350° F. Wrap each shrimp with a slice of pancetta. Lightly season with salt and pepper, and dust with flour. Thread the shrimp onto the skewers, 3 to a skewer.

■ Heat the olive oil in a large skillet, add the skewered shrimp, and sauté for a few seconds on each side. Place the skillet in the oven for 2 to 3 minutes.

■ While the shrimp bakes, sprinkle the grated cheese over the rice, toss gently, and spoon the rice onto warm plates. Remove the shrimp from the skewers and arrange them on the plates. Pour the salsa verde over the shrimp. Serve at once.

Mediterranean Calamari

MEDITERRANEAN-STYLE SQUID

SERVES 4 TO 6

INGREDIENTS

2 tablespoons olive oil	1 (6-ounce) can tomato paste
2 medium-size yellow onions, minced	1 cup dry white wine or dry vermouth
2 to 3 garlic cloves, crushed	1/8 teaspoon crushed hot red peppers
2 pounds squid (cleaned and skinned), cut into 1-inch pieces	1 tablespoon minced fresh parsley
	Salt to taste

METHOD

■ In a large saucepan, heat the olive oil. Add the onions and sauté for 8 to 10 minutes, until golden. Add the garlic and sauté for 1 minute. Add the squid, 1 cup water, and all the remaining ingredients, except the salt. Mix well, cover, and simmer for 45 to 60 minutes, stirring occasionally, until the squid is tender (the best way to tell is to eat a piece). Add salt. Serve over hot boiled rice.

Frittata alla Marinara

SEAFOOD OMELET

SERVES 6

INGREDIENTS

4 to 5 tablespoons olive oil, divided	1 pound medium shrimp in shell
1 garlic clove, minced	6 eggs
1 pound mussels, scrubbed and debearded	Minced fresh parsley
1 pound clams, scrubbed and rinsed	Salt and pepper to taste
12 oysters, scrubbed	

METHOD

▪ Heat 2 tablespoons of the oil in a large pan. Add the garlic and sauté till golden, then add the mussels, clams, and oysters. Heat until most of the shells open, discarding any that did not open. Strain the broth and return to the pot. Bring to a boil and add the shrimp. Cook the shrimp until just tender. Remove and peel the shrimp. Strain the broth and set aside.

▪ Beat the eggs with the parsley and a pinch of salt and pepper. Dilute with a tablespoon of the broth. Combine the egg mixture with the shellfish.

▪ Heat 3 tablespoons olive oil in a frying pan. Cook the egg mixture over medium heat, turning once after the eggs have begun to set.

Eel Stew

SERVES
6 TO 8

The average eel weighs 1 to 4 pounds; its meat is oily but mellow in flavor. Popular along the Mediterranean coast of Italy, they can be baked, broiled, charbroiled, pan-fried, or poached.

INGREDIENTS

2 (3-pound) eels	1 cup brown stock
2 tablespoons clarified butter	2 tablespoons red wine
3/4 pound small pearl onions	Salt and pepper to taste
6y tablespoons all-purpose flour	Minced fresh parsley

METHOD

■ Cut off the eels' heads. Wash the eels thoroughly in cold, salted water, then soak them in clean water for 15 minutes. Skin, clean, bone, and rinse them. Cut them into slices 1 1/2 inches thick, and dry the slices thoroughly.

■ Melt the butter in a large sauté pan. Add the onions and sauté until golden. Sprinkle in the flour. Stir in the stock and wine; bring to a boil. Add the eel slices and salt and pepper. Simmer gently until the eel is tender, at least 30 minutes. Arrange the eel slices and onions on a serving dish. Strain the sauce over the fish and garnish with parsley. Serve hot.

Naselli alla Marchigiana

COD IN THE STYLE OF THE MARCHES

SERVES 4

The variety of fish caught along the Marches on the Adriatic coast is astounding. As you might expect, this area is known for its fish recipes. In Italy this recipe is made with hake. I have substituted cod or any firm-fleshed fish.

INGREDIENTS

2 pounds cod fillets	About 1/2 cup dry bread crumbs
Salt and pepper to taste	4 tablespoons butter
2 shallots, finely chopped	1 anchovy, rinsed, deboned, and chopped
1 garlic clove, finally chopped	Pinch potato flour
3/4 cup olive oil, divided	1 tablespoon red wine vinegar

METHOD

■ Lay the fish fillets side by side in a bowl just big enough to hold them. Sprinkle with the salt and pepper, the shallots, and the garlic. Pour all but 2 tablespoons of the olive oil over the fish, and leave it to marinate for an hour.

■ Prepare a grill for cooking the fish.

■ Remove the fish fillets from the marinade, coat them with the bread crumbs, and sprinkle them with the remaining 2 tablespoons olive oil. Grill them on both sides over high heat.

■ While the fish is grilling, melt the butter in a small saucepan. Stir in the anchovy, potato flour, vinegar, and a little salt and pepper. Cook over low heat, mashing the pieces of the anchovy with a fork until the sauce is smooth.

■ Serve the fish with the sauce poured over.

Sogliola Certosina

FILLET OF SOLE CERTOSINA

SERVES 2

INGREDIENTS

2 to 4 tablespoons butter	1 garlic clove, crushed
4 medium-size fillets of sole (about 1 pound)	1/2 cup dry white wine
	1 (15-ounce) can plum tomatoes, chopped
3 to 4 ounces jumbo shrimp, shelled and deveined	Salt and pepper to taste
	1/2 cup whipping cream

METHOD

■ Heat the butter in a large skillet and briefly sauté the fillets on both sides to seal in the juices. Add the shrimp and garlic. Continue to sauté for 2 to 3 minutes. Add the white wine; cook until most of the liquid has evaporated. Add the tomatoes and simmer gently. Season with the salt and pepper, then stir in the cream. Simmer until the liquid is reduced. Correct the seasoning and serve.

Torte di Pesce Spada

SWORDFISH PIE

SERVES 8

A Sicilian dish. You can substitute halibut for the swordfish, if you like.

INGREDIENTS

PASTA FROLLA

4 cups all-purpose flour

3/4 cup sugar

Pinch salt

1 cup butter

4 to 5 egg yolks

Grated zest of lemon

Egg yolk

FILLING

1 tablespoon olive oil

2 medium-size onions, minced

2 tablespoons tomato paste, diluted with 2 tablespoons water

2 celery ribs, minced

3 to 4 ounces green olives, pitted and chopped

2 tablespoons capers

1 pound swordfish, finely chopped

Salt and pepper to taste

Oil for deep frying

4 to 5 small zucchini

1 egg

1/2 cup all-purpose flour

METHOD

■ In a mixing bowl, combine the flour, sugar, and salt. Cut in the butter, and work the dough until the pieces are no larger than pea-size. Make a well in the center and add the egg yolks and lemon zest. Stir with your fingers until the ingredients are well blended and the mixture forms a ball. If the dough remains too crumbly, add a little water. Wrap the dough in waxed paper, and leave it in the refrigerator for an hour.

■ To make the filling, heat the olive oil in a large sauté pan. Add the onions and sauté until they are golden brown. Add the tomato paste, celery, olives, and capers. Season the swordfish with salt and pepper and add it to the pan. Cook gently until the sauce is well reduced and the swordfish is cooked.

■ In a heavy saucepan, heat the oil for frying the zucchini. Cut the zucchini into 1/2-inch by 2-inch strips. Coat the strips with first the beaten egg, then the flour. Fry the strips in the hot oil; drain on absorbent paper.

■ Preheat the oven to 350° F.

METHOD

■ Butter and flour an 8-inch torte pan with a removable rim. Divide the pastry into thirds. Gently roll the first piece into a circle slightly larger than the pan. Place it in the pan so it covers the bottom and comes partly up the side. Lay half the swordfish mixture and half the zucchini in this bed. Roll out a second pastry circle, and cover the swordfish and zucchini with it; add another layer of swordfish and zucchini. Top with a third pastry circle, making sure it reaches the side of the pan all around. Brush egg yolk over the top.

■ Bake for 50 to 55 minutes, until the pastry is golden brown. Remove the rim of the pan and serve the pie warm.

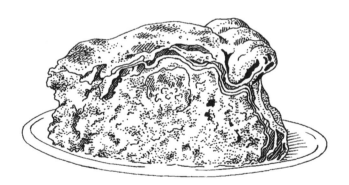

Misto di Pesce del Tirreno

MIXED FISH FROM THE TYRRHENIAN SEA

SERVES 4

INGREDIENTS

2 1/2 pounds mixed fish and shellfish	1/4 cup minced fresh parsley
1/2 cup white wine	1/4 cup minced fresh basil
1 tablespoon olive oil	1 small onion, minced
Salt and pepper to taste	

METHOD

■ Preheat the oven to 425° F.

■ Oil a baking pan large enough to hold all the seafood, and lay the seafood on it. Sprinkle the seafood with the white wine, oil, and salt and pepper. Place the pan in the oven, and braise for 10 minutes, uncovered. Remove the pan from the oven, and sprinkle the minced herbs over the seafood. Return the pan to the oven for another 5 minutes. Serve hot.

Insalata di Pasta con Frutta di Mare

PASTA SALAD WITH SEAFOOD

SERVES 6

INGREDIENTS

1 pound fusilli	1/2 pound baby clams
1/4 red onion, cut into chunks	1/2 pound cooked crabmeat
1/2 lemon	1 teaspoon chopped garlic
1 celery rib	1 teaspoon chopped fresh parsley
2 garlic cloves	1 teaspoon chopped fresh basil leaves
3 bay leaves	1 sweet red pepper, chopped
12 medium shrimp, peeled and deveined	1 green pepper, chopped
1/2 pound sea scallops	3/4 cup virgin olive oil
1/2 pound red snapper, cut into chunks	Salt and pepper to taste

METHOD

■ Cook the fusilli in plenty of boiling salted water for 7 to 8 minutes, or until it is tender but still firm. Drain the fusilli, rinse it with cold water, and drain it again.

■ Bring to a boil 1 gallon salted water with the onion, lemon, celery, garlic cloves, and bay leaves; boil for 3 minutes. Then add all the seafood, except the crabmeat, and boil for 2 minutes. Drain and let cool at room temperature.

■ Place the pasta, boiled seafood, and crabmeat in a large bowl, and mix together. Add the chopped garlic, parsley, basil, red and green peppers, and the olive oil. Add salt and pepper, mix thoroughly, and serve.

Casseruola di Pesce

FISH CASSEROLE

SERVES 1

INGREDIENTS

1/4 cup olive oil	1 garlic clove, chopped
1 fresh fish fillet	1 cup white wine
2 large shrimp, in their shells	1 cup peeled whole tomatoes
1/2 live lobster, cut into pieces	Ground red pepper to taste
4 clams	Chopped fresh parsley
Several mussels	Salt and pepper to taste

METHOD

■ In a large pan, heat the olive oil. Briefly sauté the whitefish on both sides. Add the shrimp, lobster, clams, and mussels. When the seafood is half cooked, add the garlic. Add the wine and cook to reduce it to half its original volume. Add the tomatoes and again reduce the sauce. When the seafood is fully cooked, season with the red pepper, parsley, and salt and pepper.

Salt Cod with White Wine

SERVES 4

INGREDIENTS

2 pounds salt cod	Juice of 2 lemons
1/2 cup all-purpose flour	1/4 cup chopped fresh parsley
1/2 cup olive oil	Salt and pepper
2 onions, chopped	4 green tomatoes, sliced
1 cup white wine	

METHOD

■ Soak the cod in several changes of water for 24 to 36 hours. Prepare a grill. Divide the cod into fourths. Coat each piece with flour. Lay them on the grill and cook until they are white in the center and firm to the touch. While the fish cooks, prepare the sauce. Heat the oil in a saucepan. Add the onions and sauté until golden. Add the wine, lemon juice, parsley, and salt and pepper, and cook for 10 minutes. To serve, spoon the sauce over the fish and garnish with slices of green tomato.

THE VERSATILE ITALIAN CHICKEN

▲▲▲▲▲▲▲▲▲▲▲▲▲▲▲▲▲▲

Poultry has been preferred to red meat in the Italian diet for centuries. Chicken, turkey, capons, and squabs, as well as game birds, are found on menus throughout the country.

Until recently, chicken was food only for the rich. Chickens were kept primarily for their eggs, and the flesh was eaten only when the bird was too old to be a productive layer. Nonetheless, the enormous number of distinctively Italian chicken dishes is staggering. Chicken is broiled, baked, stewed, and cooked on a spit. It is cooked with innumerable sauces that change a simple dish to an elaborate one. Chicken breasts are scallopined (boned and pounded), breaded, sautéed, and combined with a rich sauce of Marsala wine and cream. A favorite cooking method is pan-roasting.

Turkey was introduced into Europe from North America by the Spaniards in the sixteenth century. In the Lombardy and Piedmont regions of Italy, a traditional Christmas dinner is roast turkey stuffed with a mixture of chestnuts, sausage, truffles, apples, and prunes.

Pollo Ripieno all Lucana

STUFFED CHICKEN LUCANIA STYLE

SERVES 3 TO 4

INGREDIENTS

4 tablespoons lard or butter	2 1/2 pound chicken, washed and patted dry
4 to 5 chicken livers	1 to 2 sprigs fresh sage (optional)
Salt and pepper to taste	1 sprig fresh rosemary (optional)
2 eggs	
4 tablespoons grated Pecorino Romano cheese	

METHOD

■ Preheat the oven to 375° F.

■ Heat 1 tablespoon of the lard in a small pan. Add the livers and a pinch of salt and pepper and sauté gently for 5 minutes. Remove from the heat and chop the livers finely; set aside.

■ Beat the eggs. Mix the eggs with the cheese and the livers.

■ Sprinkle the cavity of the chicken with salt, and stuff it with the cheese mixture. Insert the sage and rosemary, if desired. Sew up the opening, and truss or tie the chicken. Rub the outside of the chicken with the 3 remaining tablespoons of the lard, and sprinkle with salt and freshly grated pepper. Put the chicken in a roasting pan. Roast for about 1 hour, turning the chicken occasionally and basting it with the pan juices.

■ Serve the chicken with the pan juice on the side.

Pollo all Vesuvio

CHICKEN IN THE STYLE OF VESUVIUS

SERVES 4

Today it's restaurant fare, but a friend told me he learned to make this simple chicken dish by watching his grandmother prepare it. The chicken is richly flavored with garlic and Marsala. A bit of red pepper gives it a glow that makes it worthy to be named after Vesuvius, a still-active volcano situated east of the Bay of Naples.

INGREDIENTS

2 chickens, washed and patted dry	Freshly ground black pepper to taste
1/4 cup olive oil	Ground red pepper to taste
4 garlic cloves, crushed	1/4 cup Marsala wine
4 teaspoons minced garlic	1/4 cup chicken stock
1/4 teaspoon salt	1 teaspoon finely chopped Italian parsley

METHOD

■ Preheat the oven to 450° F. Cut each chicken in half, then cut each half into 8 pieces.

■ Heat the olive oil in a heavy ovenproof skillet over high heat. Add the crushed garlic cloves and cook until lightly browned. Add the chicken pieces and fry until they are brown and crisp on both sides. Place the skillet in the oven for approximately 15 minutes. Remove the skillet from the oven, drain off the oil, and remove the garlic cloves. Add the minced garlic, salt, and black and red pepper. Place the skillet on the stove over high heat until the garlic is browned. Add the Marsala and chicken stock. Continue cooking until the wine and stock are absorbed. Garnish with the parsley and serve.

Pollo Calabrese

CHICKEN, CALABRIA STYLE

SERVES 2

INGREDIENTS

1/2 chicken, cut into serving pieces	6 tablespoons white wine
3 tablespoons olive oil	4 bay leaves
1 garlic clove, minced	1/2 teaspoon dried rosemary
1/2 cup quartered mushrooms	1/2 teaspoon dried thyme
6 green olives (not pitted)	1/4 teaspoon salt
1/4 cup butter	Freshly ground black pepper to taste

METHOD

■ Preheat the oven to 350° F. Lay the chicken pieces in a baking pan, and bake for 25 minutes. In a large pan, heat the olive oil. Add the garlic and brown over high heat. Add the chicken, mushrooms, and olives. Add the butter and white wine, and bring to a boil. Add 6 tablespoons water, the bay leaves, herbs, salt, and pepper. Boil for 2 minutes. Cover and simmer for 20 minutes. Serve.

Chicken Bianco

SERVES
3 TO 4

Here, the chicken is sautéed in a light mixture of pimento, oregano, parsley, garlic, and wine.

INGREDIENTS

1/2 cup butter	1 (8-ounce) can pimentos, sliced
3 boneless chicken breasts, cut into 1-inch slices	1 teaspoon dried oregano
	1 1/2 teaspoons minced fresh parsley
12 ounces sweet Italian sausage, sliced	3 garlic cloves, minced
2 medium-size onions, sliced	2 tablespoons white wine
1 medium-size green pepper, sliced	

METHOD

■ In a skillet, melt the butter. Add the chicken slices, sausage, onions, and green pepper and sauté. Add the pimentos, oregano, parsley, garlic, and white wine. Simmer for 8 minutes, and serve.

Sicilian Chicken with Mint and Almonds

SERVES 4

The assertive flavors of the Middle East, typical of the Sicilian kitchen, radiate from this dish.

INGREDIENTS

1/4 cup fresh mint leaves, tightly packed	1 medium-size lemon
1 large garlic clove	Salt
3 1/2 pound chicken, quartered	1/3 cup blanched whole almonds
3 tablespoons lemon juice	2 tablespoons white wine vinegar
3 1/2 tablespoons olive oil, divided	1 tablespoon minced fresh mint leaves
1/4 teaspoon freshly ground pepper	Mint sprigs

METHOD

■ Mince together the 1/4 cup mint leaves and the garlic clove. Rub the chicken pieces with the mixture. Arrange the chicken pieces in a single layer in a shallow dish.

■ In a small bowl, combine the lemon juice, 1 tablespoon of the olive oil, and the pepper. Pour the marinade over the chicken and turn the pieces to coat them evenly. Cover the dish and refrigerate it for at least 5 hours, or overnight.

■ Using a sharp knife, cut very thin strips of the rind from the lemon, and boil them in water to cover for 5 minutes. Drain.

■ Remove the chicken from the dish. Scrape the mint mixture off the chicken and into the marinade. Reserve the marinade. Pat the chicken dry, and salt it lightly.

■ Heat the remaining 2 1/2 tablespoons olive oil in a large heavy skillet over medium heat. Add the almonds and sauté until they are golden, stirring frequently. Remove them with a slotted spoon. Add the chicken to the skillet, and brown it well on all sides. Stir in the vinegar, scraping up the browned bits from the bottom of the pan. Add the lemon peel and the reserved marinade. Reduce the heat, cover, and cook for 15 minutes. Add the almonds and 1 tablespoon mint leaves. Cover and cook, turning occasionally, until the chicken is tender, 10 to 15 minutes. (Add water if necessary to prevent the chicken from sticking to the pan.)

■ Transfer the chicken to a heated platter, and pour the pan juices over. Garnish with mint sprigs, and serve.

Baked Chicken Giovanna

SERVES 4 TO 6

A simple, tasty chicken dish.

INGREDIENTS

MARINADE

3/4 cup olive oil

1 cup sherry

1 tablespoon crushed garlic

1 tablespoon dried oregano

1 tablespoon salt

1/2 tablespoon black pepper

CHICKEN

3-pound chicken, cut into pieces

Paprika

METHOD

■ Mix the marinade ingredients. Place the chicken in a shallow baking pan and pour the marinade over it. Let stand for 30 minutes.

■ Preheat the oven to 350° F. Bake the chicken for 1 hour. Turn the pieces after 30 minutes. About 5 minutes before the chicken is done, sprinkle it lightly with paprika.

Chicken Cacciatore

SERVES 4

In this famous dish from central Italy, the chicken is simmered with mushrooms, onions, celery, carrots, herbs and sometimes tomatoes.

INGREDIENTS

2-pound to 3-pound chicken, cut into pieces

Flour

1/2 cup olive oil

1/2 cup minced onion

1 garlic clove, chopped

1 cup chopped celery

1 large green bell pepper, chopped

1 (15-ounce) can tomatoes, crushed

1 (8-ounce) can tomato sauce

1/4 cup chopped fresh parsley

1 bay leaf

1 (4-ounce) can button mushrooms

METHOD

■ Dredge the chicken in flour. Heat oil in a large skillet, add the chicken, and brown on all sides. Remove the chicken pieces. Brown the onion, celery, and bell pepper. Stir in the tomatoes and the tomato sauce. Return the chicken to the pan and add parsley and bay leaf. Simmer for 30 minutes. Add mushrooms, and simmer for 10 minutes.

Petto di Pollo Vicontessa

VICONTESSA'S BREAST OF CHICKEN

SERVES 4

This is a family recipe from Abbiategrasso, Milan. Drink dry white wine with it.

INGREDIENTS

3 tablespoons olive oil	6 tablespoons Marsala wine
1 cup sliced button mushrooms	6 tablespoons chicken broth
2 tablespoons butter	Salt and pepper to taste
2 whole chicken breasts, boned, skinned, and pounded into 12-inch-thick scallops	2 tablespoons julienned pimento
	Juice of 1/2 lemon
3 tablespoons cognac	3/4 cup whipping cream

METHOD

■ Heat 3 tablespoons of the olive oil in a large frying pan. Add the mushrooms and sauté. Remove the mushrooms and set aside.

■ And butter to the pan and heat almost to the smoking point. Slip the chicken pieces into the pan and brown them on both sides. When they are golden brown, pour off the fat. Then pour the cognac and Marsala wine into the pan. With a match, light the liquor and flame the chicken until the fire goes out. Add the broth. Season with the salt and pepper. Reduce the liquid by half. Add the mushrooms, pimento, lemon juice, and cream. Simmer for a few minutes, until the sauce is a desirable consistency. Serve.

Petti di Pollo al Spinacci e Formaggio

BREASTS OF CHICKEN WITH SPINACH AND CHEESE

SERVES 4

INGREDIENTS

4 large skinless, boneless chicken breasts (or 8 small)	2 garlic cloves, minced
	Salt, pepper, and paprika to taste
1 pound spinach, chopped	Juice of 1/2 lemon
12 to 14 ounces Parmesan cheese, grated	1 cup dry white wine
1/4 cup olive oil	Chopped Italian parsley

METHOD

■ With a sharp knife, slice the breasts lengthwise to form a pocket. Fill each breast with a portion of the spinach and the Parmesan cheese. In a large skillet, heat the oil. Add the chicken and brown it. Sprinkle with the garlic, salt, pepper, and paprika. Turn a few times, and add the lemon juice and wine. Cover and cook for 30 to 35 minutes. Serve garnished with parsley.

Philip's Chicken Angelo

SERVES 6

INGREDIENTS

3 boneless chicken breasts, cut into pieces	Juice of a small lemon
Flour	2 garlic cloves, minced
6 tablespoons clarified butter, divided	1 cup sliced mushrooms
Dash dried oregano	6 (canned or frozen) artichoke hearts, quartered
Dash dried basil	
Salt and pepper to taste	1 tablespoon chopped fresh parsley
1/3 cup dry white wine	3/4 cup brandy

METHOD

■ Dredge the chicken in flour. Heat 4 tablespoons of the butter in a skillet add the chicken and brown. Add the herbs and seasoning. Add the remaining butter, wine, lemon juice, and garlic. Simmer for 4 to 5 minutes. Add the mushrooms, artichoke hearts, and parsley. Cook 3 minutes. Turn the heat to high; add the brandy. Ignite it. Let the flames die down and serve.

Involtini di Petti di Pollo

STUFFED CHICKEN BREASTS

SERVES 6

Chicken breasts are stuffed with cheese and asparagus and smothered with a mushroom cream sauce.

INGREDIENTS

12 skinless, boneless chicken breasts, cut in half	1/2 cup minced fresh parsley
12 thin slices prosciutto	Olive oil
3/4 pound Bel Paese cheese, cut into 12 oblongs	Flour
	MARSALA SAUCE
24 asparagus spears, blanched 1 minute and trimmed to 4 inches	1 pound mushrooms, thinly sliced
	3/4 cup dry Marsala wine
3/4 pound (total) Parmesan and Romano cheese, grated and mixed	6 cups whipping cream
	Salt and pepper to taste

METHOD

■ Pound the chicken between sheets of waxed paper to a thickness of 1/4 inch. Lay them shiny side down on the counter, and cover each breast with 1 prosciutto slice. Set a Bel Paese cheese oblong in the center, and place 2 pieces of asparagus beside the cheese. Sprinkle with about 3 tablespoons of the Parmesan-Romano mixture, then with the parsley. Tightly roll up the breasts.

■ Preheat the oven to 350° F.

■ In a large heavy skillet, heat a thin layer of oil over medium heat. Dredge the chicken rolls in the flour, shaking off any excess. Arrange the rolls seam side down in the skillet and brown them on both sides. Transfer them to a baking sheet. Pour the oil from the pan over them. (Do not wash the skillet.) Bake the chicken until it is tender, about 15 minutes.

■ While the chicken bakes, set the skillet over high heat, and add the mushrooms and Marsala wine. Tilt the pan, heat the wine and ignite it with a match. When the flame subsides, boil the liquid until it is reduced by half. Add the cream and boil the sauce until it is reduced to a desirable consistency. Season with salt and pepper.

■ Spoon the Marsala sauce over the chicken and serve.

Rollatini di Pollo Don Fosco

FOSCO'S STUFFED CHICKEN BREAST

SERVES 4

A recipe that originated in the Tuscany region of Italy.

INGREDIENTS

4 skinless, boneless chicken breasts, cut in half	1/4 teaspoon freshly ground black pepper
1/2 pound ground pork	Dried basil, oregano, and sage to taste
1/2 medium-size onion, chopped	1/4 cup cooked chopped spinach
1/3 cup crumbled cooked bacon bits	2 teaspoons butter, melted
2 garlic cloves, chopped	Salt and pepper to taste
1 egg	1/2 cup dry Marsala wine
1/2 cup fresh white bread crumbs	1 cup beef or chicken stock
1/2 teaspoon salt	Chopped fresh parsley

METHOD

■ Pound the chicken breasts between sheets of waxed paper to a thickness of 1/4 inch.

■ Preheat the oven to 400° F.

■ In a skillet, fry the ground pork. Add the onion, bacon, and garlic, and cook until all are brown. Drain the fat from the skillet. Stir in the egg, bread crumbs, salt and pepper, herbs, and spinach. Mix well.

■ Place equal portions of stuffing on each chicken breast. Roll up the breasts, and secure the rolls with toothpicks. Place the rolls, seam side down, in a greased baking pan, and brush them with the butter. Sprinkle them with salt and pepper. Pour the Marsala wine over, and bake for 35 to 40 minutes.

■ Remove the pan from the oven and the rolls from the pan. Stir the brown stock into the pan juices, and return the pan to the oven for 5 more minutes. Replace the rolls in the resulting sauce, and sparkle them with the parsley. Serve the rolls with the sauce and mashed potatoes or polenta.

Pollo alla Fiorentina

FLORENCE-STYLE CHICKEN

SERVES 6

INGREDIENTS

2 whole chickens, cut in half	1/2 cup butter
1/4 pound ground Italian sausage	2 tablespoons chopped shallots
1/4 pound spinach, chopped, cooked, and drained	Dash dry vermouth
	Salt and pepper to taste

METHOD

■ Remove the chicken wings (reserve them for stock or another use). Carefully separate each chicken breast half from the bone, all the way down to the thigh. Roll back the meat on the thigh to remove the thigh bone without puncturing the skin. This will leave only the drumstick bone attached to the meat.

■ In a small skillet, cook the Italian sausage; drain off the fat. Stir in the spinach.

■ In a separate pan, melt the butter. Sauté the shallots lightly, and stir in the sausage-spinach mixture. Add the vermouth, salt, and pepper. Mix well. Let the stuffing cool.

■ Preheat the oven to 400° F.

■ Place a portion of the stuffing on the boned side of each chicken half. Mold the meat around the stuffing, overlapping the sides, to form a pear shape, with the drumstick sticking up. Place the chicken halves seam side down on a greased roasting pan, and bake until they are done, about 1 hour. Serve.

Pollo alla Gorgonzola

CHICKEN WITH GORGONZOLA CHEESE

SERVES 2

INGREDIENTS

1/4 pound Gorgonzola cheese, crumbled	1/3 cup sliced mushrooms
White wine	3/4 cup cream
6 ounces cubed chicken breast	5 tablespoons grated Parmesan cheese
Flour	Salt and pepper to taste
1/4 cup butter	2 1/2 ounces fettuccine
2 scallions, sliced	Chopped fresh parsley

METHOD

■ Begin heating the water for the pasta. Place the Gorgonzola in a glass or ceramic bowl and cover with the white wine. Set aside.

■ Dredge the chicken in the flour; shake off any excess. In a skillet, melt the butter. Add the chicken and sauté for 1 minute. Add the scallions and mushrooms and sauté until the mushrooms are limp, about 5 minutes. Add the Gorgonzola mixture, the cream, Parmesan cheese, and salt and pepper. Heat, stirring, until the cream thickens. Reduce the heat to very low.

■ When the cream has thickened and the water for the pasta has reached a full boil, drop the fettuccine into the boiling water. Boil until the pasta is tender but still firm; drain. Place the cooked fettuccine on a platter, top with the chicken. Garnish with the parsley and serve.

MEATS, ITALIAN STYLE

▲▲▲▲▲▲▲▲▲▲▲▲▲▲▲▲▲▲

Milk-fed veal is probably the most popular meat in Italy. Veal can be sautéed, braised, fried, stewed, roasted, or poached. Veal shank is an inexpensive cut of meat, and braising makes it tender enough to cut with a fork. The shoulder cut of veal is best for stews. Boned breast of veal is excellent for veal roast, stuffed and rolled before pan-roasting.

Beef is not a favorite with Italians for two reasons: The cow is prized for her milk and the ox for his labor. But although relatively few cattle in Italy are raised for their meat, the country produces some of the best in the world. The most common way of cooking beef, regardless of the cut, is slowly in pot roasts and stews with wine, herbs, and vegetables.

Italians eat a considerable amount of pork, mostly in the form of sausage and ham. In many northern Italian dishes, pork is barely visible, yet vital to the flavor. Traditionally, lamb is synonymous with Easter and spring in the Italian home.

Veal Scalopine Mamma Chiara

SERVES 4

This recipe originated on the Isle of Capri.

INGREDIENTS

1/4 cup butter	2 ounces prosciutto, chopped
9 thin slices veal	3 tablespoons whipping cream
2 cups finely diced assorted cheeses (Fontina, Bel Paese, mozzarella, Parmesan, etc.)	1/2 cup pâté de foie gras
	Salt and pepper to taste
	Parmesan cheese

METHOD

■ Preheat the oven to 400° F. Melt the butter in a heavy skillet. Add the veal slices and sauté them briefly on both sides. Remove the pan from the heat. Lay on top of each veal slice one slice smoked ham, 1/4 cup of the mushrooms, some zucchini slices, and a sprinkle of parsley; top with 1/4 of the mozzarella. Bake for about 15 minutes, or until the cheese melts. Transfer the veal to hot plates, and sprinkle with a bit of minced garlic and rosemary.

Scalopine di Vitello alla Toscana

VEAL SCALLOPS FROM TUSCANY

SERVES 4 TO 6

A northern Italian dish found primarily in Tuscany and Emilia-Romagna, where fresh herbs are widely used in cooking.

INGREDIENTS

1 pound veal scallops	2 fresh sage leaves, minced
1/2 cup all-purpose flour	6 fresh basil leaves, minced
1/4 cup melted butter	Pinch fresh thyme leaves, minced
1/4 pound mushrooms, chopped	1/3 cup Marsala wine
1 garlic clove, minced	Salt and pepper to taste
1 shallot, minced	2 tablespoons whipping cream

METHOD

■ Dust the veal scallops with flour. Melt the butter. Add the veal scallops and cook them very briefly on each side. Drain off all the fat from the pan. Add the mushrooms, garlic, shallot, herbs, wine, salt, and pepper. Heat until the wine is reduced. Add the whipping cream, stir, and serve.

Veal Piccata

SERVES 4

INGREDIENTS

1 pound veal scallops, cut in 8 slices, pounded	1/4 cup olive oil
Flour	2 ounces grated Parmesan cheese
2 eggs, beaten	Finely minced parsley
Fine dry bread crumbs	1/4 cup butter
	3 garlic cloves, minced

METHOD

■ Dust each slice of veal with flour. Dip into the eggs and then into the bread crumbs. Heat the oil in a heavy skillet. Add the veal. Reduce the heat, and fry it gently on both sides, until lightly browned. Place the scallops on a hot serving dish and sprinkle them with Parmesan cheese and parsley. Discard the oil, and add the butter to the same pan. Melt the butter. When it begins to foam add the garlic and stir. Remove the skillet from the heat and coat the scallops with the garlic butter.

Fagottini alla Bruno

BRUNO'S SMALL BUNDLES

SERVES 4

This recipe originated in Tuscany.

INGREDIENTS

8 thin slices cooked ham	1 tablespoon olive oil
8 veal scallops, pounded	2 tablespoons butter
8 oblong pieces Parmesan cheese	1 tablespoon white wine
Flour	

METHOD

■ Place 1 slice of ham on each slice of veal. In the center of each piece of ham, place 1 piece of Parmesan cheese. Carefully roll up each veal scallop and secure the roll with toothpicks. Dredge each roll in flour. Combine the olive oil and butter in a heavy skillet over low heat. Cook the veal rolls, turning them frequently, for about 15 minutes. When they are done, sprinkle them with the wine. Let the wine evaporate.

Saltimbocca alla Romana

"JUMP IN YOUR MOUTH," ROMAN-STYLE

SERVES 6 TO 8

INGREDIENTS

2 pounds veal scallops, pounded and cut into 8 pieces	1/8 teaspoon freshly ground black pepper
2 tablespoons minced fresh sage or 1 teaspoon dried sage	1/4 pound paper-thin prosciutto slices
	3 to 4 tablespoons butter or margarine
	1/4 cup dry white wine

METHOD

■ Sprinkle one side of each veal slice with some sage and pepper. Top with a slice of prosciutto, and secure the prosciutto with a toothpick.

■ In a large skillet melt the butter. Brown the veal quickly on both sides. Transfer it to a heated platter, remove the toothpicks. Pour the wine into the skillet and let the wine boil, uncovered, for 1 to 2 minutes, scraping up any brown bits with a wooden spoon. Pour the sauce over the veal and serve.

Veal Parmigiana

SERVES 4

INGREDIENTS

3 to 4 eggs	1/2 cup oil
1 cup milk	4 slices prosciutto
1 pound veal scallops, pounded	2 tomatoes, sliced
Salt and pepper to taste	8 slices mozzarella cheese
Flour	Paprika
Dry bread crumbs	

METHOD

■ Preheat the oven to 400° F. Beat the eggs and milk together. Season the veal with salt and pepper. Dip the scallops into the flour, then into the egg mixture, and finally into the bread crumbs. In a heavy skillet, heat the oil. Add the veal and brown on both sides. Place the scallops on a baking sheet. Top each with a slice of prosciutto, 2 slices of tomato, 2 slices of mozzarella cheese, and paprika, then place the baking sheet in the oven for 5 minutes.

Veal alla Pingolo

SERVES 4 TO 6

INGREDIENTS

5 cooked chicken livers	3 bacon slices, cut into small pieces
2 sweet Italian sausages, cooked and skinned	Fresh sage leaves
1 garlic clove, minced	Flour
1 tablespoon minced fresh parsley	1/4 cup butter
2 to 3 tablespoons grated Parmesan cheese	Salt to taste
2 egg yolks	1/2 cup dry white wine
1 1/2 pounds veal scallops, pounded	1/2 cup chicken stock

METHOD

■ Process the first five ingredients into a paste. Spread some on each scallop. Tightly roll them up. Put a bacon piece and sage leaf on top of each roll and secure with toothpicks. Dust the rolls with flour. Melt the butter in a skillet. Add the rolls and brown. Add the salt and wine and simmer. Add the stock and simmer for 20 minutes.

Veal Bolognese

SERVES 4

INGREDIENTS

8 thin slices baked or boiled ham	1 cup milk
4 veal scallops, cut in half	Flour
8 slices mozzarella cheese	Dry bread crumbs
1/2 cup ricotta cheese, divided	1/2 cup vegetable oil
4 eggs	

METHOD

■ Lay a slice of ham on each half-scallop. Pound the ham and veal together. Lay mozzarella on each slice. Spread 1 tablespoon of the ricotta over each. Beat the eggs and milk together. Roll up the scallops, and secure with toothpicks. Dredge in flour, dip in the egg mixture, and cover with bread crumbs. Heat the oil in a heavy skillet. Sauté until golden brown.

125

Scallopini al Vermouth

VEAL SCALLOPS WITH VERMOUTH

SERVES 4

INGREDIENTS

2 pounds veal scallops	1 teaspoon salt
1/2 cup flour	1/4 teaspoon freshly ground black pepper
1/4 cup butter	1/4 cup dry vermouth
1/2 cup chopped red bell peppers	

METHOD

■ Dredge the veal in the flour, shaking off the excess. Melt the butter in a skillet. When the butter is hot, add the scallopini and the peppers. Cook the fillets over high heat for 2 minutes on each side, shaking the pan a few times. Sprinkle the meat with salt and pepper and pour the vermouth over it. Reduce the heat, and cook the fillets 1 minute more on each side for rare meat, or longer if you desire.

■ Arrange the fillets on a hot serving dish and pour the sauce from the pan over them.

Ossobuco alla Milanese

VEAL SHANKS IN THE STYLE OF MILAN

SERVES 6

This dish originated in Milan, where it was prepared for that city's aristocracy. The veal shanks are stewed very slowly in a mixture of tomatoes, wine, and herbs. The essence of the dish is the bone marrow, which you dig out of the bone with a special little fork that is usually provided. This dish is usually served with a generous helping of rice.

INGREDIENTS

6 (2-inch) slices veal shank, each tied round with a string

Flour

1/2 cup butter

1 pound button mushrooms, sliced

1 cup dry white wine

1 1/2 cups peeled Italian tomatoes

Salt and pepper to taste

1/2 cup boiling veal or beef broth

Sprig of oregano

METHOD

■ Dredge the veal shanks in flour.

■ Put the butter into a heavy casserole that has a tight-fitting lid and is just large enough to contain the veal in 1 layer. Heat the butter; when it foams, add the veal. Sear the veal on both sides, then remove the veal shanks and keep them hot. Add the mushrooms and sauté for 2 minutes. Return the veal to the casserole, add the wine, and let it boil. When the wine is reduced, add the tomatoes. Stir gently, adding the salt and pepper. Add the boiling broth, stir a little more, then cover the casserole and reduce the heat. Simmer gently for 2 hours.

■ Put the meat on a serving dish and pour the pan juices over. Garnish with the oregano.

Osso di Vitello Stracotto

BRAISED VEAL CHOPS

SERVES 4

A tasty meal for guests that does not involve a lot of last-minute work in the kitchen. The chops can be served with the sauce on the side.

INGREDIENTS

1/2 cup olive oil	4 garlic cloves, minced
4 veal rib chops, bone in (about 1 pound total)	1 cup dry white wine
Flour	1 teaspoon whole black peppercorns
2 to 3 sprigs fresh rosemary	Salt to taste

METHOD

■ Preheat the oven to 300° F.

■ Gently heat the oil in a heavy ovenproof pan. Dredge the chops in flour, add them to the pan, and brown them on both sides. Add the rosemary, garlic, and wine, and heat until the wine evaporates. Add the peppercorns, 1 quart water, and a little salt. Stir to mix the ingredients, then transfer the dish to the oven.

■ Bake, uncovered, for about 2 hours, adding water if necessary. When done, the meat will be a nice brown color, and it will rest in a little sauce. Serve with a wine such as Montepulciano d'Abruzzo.

Costata di Manza al Barolo

BONED RIB OF BEEF IN BAROLO WINE

SERVES 6 TO 8

INGREDIENTS

3-pound boned beef rib roast	4 to 5 black peppercorns
1 onion, quartered	1 liter Barolo red wine
1 carrot, sliced	2 tablespoons lard or butter
1 celery rib, chopped	1/4 cup butter
1 bay leaf	1 teaspoon potato flour or cornstarch
Salt	

METHOD

■ Combine the meat, onion, carrot, celery, bay leaf, salt, and peppercorns in a large bowl. Pour the wine over all. Allow the meat to marinate for 24 hours, turning it occasionally.

■ Remove the meat from the marinade, and carefully pat it dry. Reserve the marinade. With a string, tie the meat into a round.

■ Strain the marinade into a saucepan, and boil it over fairly high heat until it is reduced by half.

■ Heat the lard in a pan that is large enough to hold the meat and that has a tight-fitting lid. As the fat begins to melt, add the butter. Stir until the butter is melted. Add the meat, and brown it on all sides. Season the meat with salt and pour the reduced wine over it. Cover the pan, and cook the meat over low heat for about 2 hours, or until it is very tender. (You should be able to eat it with a fork or, even, a spoon.) Transfer the meat to a heated serving dish, and keep it hot.

■ Skim the fat from the sauce and bring it to a boil again. Mix the potato flour or cornstarch to a thin paste with a little water and stir into the boiling sauce. Cook, stirring constantly, for 5 minutes. Pour a little of the sauce over the meat, and serve the rest separately.

Filetto alla Fiorentina

BEEF FILLET FROM FLORENCE

SERVES 4

INGREDIENTS

4 tablespoons olive oil, divided

1 carrot, minced

1 onion, minced

1 celery rib, minced

2 garlic cloves, minced

1 to 2 ounces chicken livers, minced

1/2 cup red wine

2 1/2 to 3 pounds beef fillet, sliced 1 to 2 inches thick

1/4 pound mushrooms, minced

1 cup peeled, seeded, and puréed or chopped tomatoes

Salt and pepper to taste

1/2 cup beef stock

METHOD

■ Heat 3 tablespoons of the olive oil in a heavy pan. Add the carrot, onion, celery, and garlic, and sauté them until they soften. Add the chicken livers, and cook until they are done. Add the red wine; simmer until the wine has evaporated.

■ In a heavy pan with a lid, heat the remaining 1 tablespoon olive oil. Brown the beef slices on both sides for a few minutes. Add the wine-simmered livers and vegetables, the mushrooms, tomato purée, salt and pepper, beef stock, and 1/2 cup water. Cover the pan and cook slowly for about 30 minutes.

Olivette della Casa

HOUSE-SPECIAL MEAT ROLLS

SERVES 6

I found this delicious dish in Padua.

INGREDIENTS

1/4 cup fresh or stale bread cubes (1/2-inch pieces)	1/4 cup fresh bread crumbs
Milk	1 1/2 pounds ground beef (not too lean)
1 egg, beaten	3/4 cup grated mozzarella cheese
1 (8-ounce) can plum tomatoes, puréed, divided	1/4 cup grated Parmesan cheese
	2 tablespoons dried parsley

METHOD

■ Preheat the oven to 350° F.

■ Soak the bread pieces in milk. Drain off the excess milk.

™ In a large bowl, combine the egg, 1/3 cup of the tomato purée, the bread crumbs, and the bread pieces. Mix in the beef. Mold the mixture into a square or rectangular loaf about 3/4 inch thick.

■ In a small bowl, combine 1/2 cup of the mozzarella cheese, the Parmesan cheese, and the parsley. Spoon the cheese mixture onto the center of the meat, leaving a 1-inch border of meat all around. Roll up the meat, pressing the edges to seal the roll.

■ Place the roll seam side down on a baking dish. Bake, uncovered, for about 30 minutes, or until the meat is nearly done. Spoon the remaining tomato purée over the meat roll, and continue baking for a few minutes. Sprinkle the top with the remaining 1/4 cup mozzarella cheese, and bake a little longer, until the cheese melts.

■ Remove the meat roll from the oven and cut it so the mozzarella filling appears in the center of each round slice. Serve hot.

Stracotto al Chianti Classico

BRAISED BEEF IN CHIANTI

SERVES 4

This is a recipe passed down from the Medici family. A *stracotto* is quite similar and sometimes identical to a *stufato*. Both are meat that is cooked slowly in either wine or tomatoes.

INGREDIENTS

Olive oil	1 bottle Chianti
1 onion, minced	2-pound boneless chuck roast
2 garlic cloves	1 carrot, chopped
1/3 cup pine nuts	1 small green pepper, chopped
1/4 cup blanched almonds	Salt and black pepper to taste
1/3 cup raisins	2 cups beef broth

METHOD

■ Preheat the oven to 325° F.

■ In a saucepan, heat 1 tablespoon olive oil. Add the onion and sauté until soft.

■ In a mortar or processor, pound the garlic, pine nuts, and almonds with a little oil to make a paste. Add the raisins and pound. Add the whole mixture to the pan with the sautéed onion. Stir in the Chianti.

■ Tie the pot roast with string to hold it together.

■ In a heavy skillet, heat enough olive oil to just cover the bottom of the pan. When the oil is quite hot, add the meat. Brown it well on all sides, then remove it and set it aside.

■ In the same pan over moderate heat, sauté the carrot and green pepper. Season with salt and pepper.

■ Combine the roast in a roasting pan with the sautéed vegetables and the beef broth. Cover the pan and place it in the oven. Bake for 2 hours, basting frequently with the wine-raisin sauce. When the meat is done, the juices will have turned nearly a caramel color.

Todd's Special

SERVES
8 TO 10
GENEROUSLY

A beef sirloin, sausage, and spinach dish served throughout Italy and particularly enjoyed in Turin.

INGREDIENTS

3 cups red wine	2 pounds Italian sausages, sweet or hot
2 cups olive oil	1 (10-ounce) package frozen chopped spinach
3 tablespoons butter	
2 medium-size onions, chopped	1/3 pound Parmesan cheese, grated
1 whole garlic bulb, the cloves separated and peeled	3 (4-ounce) cans button mushrooms, sliced
	3 eggs, beaten
2 pounds beef (preferably sirloin), diced	2 pounds linguine, cooked (optional)
Salt and pepper to taste	

METHOD

■ Heat the wine. Keep warm.

■ In a heavy, deep pan, heat the oil and butter. Add the onions and garlic cloves and sauté until they are soft; then add the diced beef. Sprinkle salt and pepper over the meat as it browns. When the meat has browned, add the wine.

■ In another pan, brown the sausages.

■ While the sausages cook, add the spinach to the beef mixture. Stir frequently as the spinach thaws; continue heating and stirring until it is cooked.

■ When the sausages are done, remove them from the skillet and slice them 1/4 inch thick. Return the sausage to the beef mixture. Blend in the cheese well, then add the mushrooms. Mix in the eggs just before serving.

■ Serve Todd's Special over fresh linguine or by itself. A dry red Italian wine is a must with this dish.

Fegato Burro Salvia

CALF'S LIVER WITH SAGE AND BUTTER

SERVES 4

A very simple dish which originated in Tuscany, a region known for the simplicity of its cuisine. The secret to success in this dish is to skin the liver carefully and slice it very thin.

INGREDIENTS

12 very thin slices calf's liver, freshly skinned

1/2 pound unsalted butter

12 fresh sage leaves

Salt to taste

METHOD

- Heat a heavy skillet.

- In a separate pan, melt the butter and add the sage Do not let the butter burn.

- While the butter melts, sprinkle the liver on both sides with salt. When the skillet is as hot as possible, place the liver slices in it. Turn them after 30 seconds, heat 30 seconds more, and then immediately transfer the liver to a warm platter. Liberally coast the slices with the sage butter.

- This dish goes well with boiled fresh spinach and mashed potatoes.

Agnello Scoytadito

LAMB

SERVES 2 TO 4   **A**n old Roman recipe.

INGREDIENTS

4 tablespoons butter, divided	Salt and pepper to taste
1 onion, chopped	1/4 cup whiskey, heated
1/2 pound mushrooms, sliced	1/2 cup light cream
1/4 pound tomatoes, peeled and chopped	1/2 cup beef stock
1 pound lamb fillet, cut into 1-inch strips	Mashed potatoes
1 tablespoon paprika	Parsley
1 garlic clove, crushed (optional)	Watercress

METHOD

■ Melt 2 tablespoons of the butter in a heavy skillet. Add the onion and sauté until it is soft but not brown. Add the mushrooms and tomatoes, and sauté for a few minutes. Remove the pan from the heat.

■ In a separate pan, melt the remaining 2 tablespoons butter. When the butter is hot, add the lamb strips. Sauté the lamb until the juices are sealed in. Add the paprika, garlic, and salt and pepper. Continue to cook for 10 minutes, stirring constantly.

■ Pour the whiskey over the lamb and ignite the liquor with a match. Let the flame subside, then quickly add the cream, beef stock, and sautéed vegetables. Cook for a few minutes more, stirring constantly, until the sauce is well mixed and warmed through.

■ Serve on a platter inside a border of piped mashed potatoes. Garnish with parsley and watercress.

Coniglio al Fiori di Finocchio

RABBIT BAKED WITH FLOWERS OF FENNEL

SERVES 4

In this country, flowers of the wild fennel are not commercially available, but you can easily find the seeds in the spice shelves of the supermarket and grind them with a mortar and pestle.

In Siena, this dish was served with puréed potatoes mixed with parsley, butter, a touch of nutmeg, and grated Parmesan cheese.

INGREDIENTS

BROWN SAUCE

2 pounds veal bones

2 carrots, peeled

1/4 cup chopped onion

1/2 pound fresh tomatoes

2 tablespoons tomato paste

3 liters white wine

Salt to taste

RABBIT

Saddle of rabbit (from the base of the neck to the top of the thigh)

Salt and pepper to taste

1/2 ounce flowers of fennel or 3 table-spoons freshly ground fennel seeds

2 to 4 tablespoons butter

METHOD

■ In a large pot, combine the veal bones, carrots, onion, tomatoes, tomato paste, and 3 quarts of water. Cook over low heat for 7 hours, occasionally skimming off the fat and adding water as necessary to keep the bones covered. Strain the sauce. Over low heat, reduce the sauce to half its original volume.

■ In another saucepan, boil the wine to evaporate the alcohol. Reduce the wine by half, and add it to the brown sauce. Cook the sauce for several minutes and season it with salt.

■ Preheat the oven to 325° F.

■ Sprinkle the rabbit with salt, pepper, and fennel flowers or seeds. In an ovenproof pan, heat the butter. Sauté the saddle of rabbit over medium heat, taking care not to burn the butter.

■ Transfer the pan to the oven and bake for 25 minutes. Remove the rabbit, and drain off the fat, taking care not to remove the fennel flowers. Bone the saddle. Slice the meat, and place it on a heated platter. Cover it with the hot sauce and serve.

VEGETABLES & SALADS

▲▲▲▲▲▲▲▲▲▲▲▲▲▲▲▲▲▲

Vegetables and salads are given considerable importance and careful treatment in Italian cuisine. Most often they are served as separate courses after the meal.

Eggplant is very popular in Italy, particularly in the South, where Eggplant Parmigiana was invented. Indeed, you will encounter eggplant prepared in countless ways if you eat your way through the South.

Other vegetables a traveler is likely to encounter in Italy include beans, lentils, asparagus, artichokes, celery, fennel, bell peppers, spinach, potatoes, salad greens, and, of course, tomatoes.

Eggplant Parmigiana

SERVES 4

The classic Sicilian eggplant dish.

INGREDIENTS

1/2 cup (or more) dry bread crumbs	1 large or 2 small eggplants, peeled and cut into slices no more than 1/4 inch thick
Salt, pepper, and dried oregano to taste	
1 egg (or more), beaten	2 cups Marinara Sauce (page 41)
1 or 2 tablespoons milk	1/2 pound mozzarella cheese
1/4 cup olive oil	Parmesan cheese

METHOD

- Season the bread crumbs with salt, pepper, and oregano.

- In a bowl, mix 1 egg with 1 tablespoon milk.

- Preheat the oven to 350° F.

- In a skillet, heat the olive oil over high heat. When the oil is very hot, reduce the heat to medium-high. Dip the eggplant slices into the milk-egg mixture, then into the seasoned bread crumbs. Fry the slices, a few at time, for 3 to 4 minutes on each side, or until they are lightly browned. Reserve the fried slices on a paper-towel-lined platter until all are done. You may need additional seasoned bread crumbs and milk-egg mixture depending on the number of eggplant slices you have.

- In a shallow casserole, spread several tablespoons of the tomato sauce. Cover the sauce with a layer of eggplant slices, brush the eggplant with tomato sauce, and sprinkle mozzarella cheese over the sauce. Add another layer of eggplant, more sauce, and more cheese, and continue layering the ingredients until you've used all the eggplant. The top layer should be cheese. Place the casserole in the oven and bake for 30 minutes, or until the cheese is bubbly and lightly browned.

- Offer Parmesan cheese at the table for sprinkling.

Eggplant Sorrentino

SERVES 6

INGREDIENTS

Olive oil or vegetable oil	18 ounces ricotta cheese
6 thick slices eggplant (from the center of a large eggplant)	Salt and pepper
	Paprika
Flour	Minced fresh parsley
1 egg, beaten	Grated Parmesan cheese
6 thin slices mozzarella cheese	Marinara Sauce (see page 41)
6 thin slices cooked ham	Grated mozzarella cheese

METHOD

■ Preheat the oven to 450° F.

■ Heat enough oil to come 1 inch up the side of a skillet.

■ Lightly flour the eggplant slices, then dip them in the egg. When the oil is hot, fry the eggplant slices just until they are golden. Place them on paper towels to drain off the excess oil.

■ When the eggplant has cooled, place atop each slice 1 slice mozzarella cheese, 1 slice cooked ham, 3 ounces (a little more than 1/3 cup) ricotta cheese, a pinch each of salt, pepper, paprika, and parsley, and some grated Parmesan cheese. Then roll each slice with its topping and secure the roll with toothpicks.

■ Spread some Marinara Sauce on the bottom of a casserole dish and arrange the eggplant rolls on top of sauce. Top them with more Marinara Sauce, and sprinkle mozzarella cheese over. Bake for 10 to 15 minutes, until the cheese is melted and bubbly. Serve.

Eggplant della Mamma

SERVES 4

Mamma Montesano's interesting version of stuffed eggplant.

INGREDIENTS

2 medium-size eggplants	Pinch ground red pepper
1/2 cup olive oil	3 tablespoons chopped fresh parsley
1/2 pound sweet Italian sausage, diced	1 cup fresh bread crumbs
1 onion, minced	Salt and pepper to taste
3 garlic cloves, minced	1 1/2 cups grated fontina or mozzarella cheese
1/2 cup white wine	
6 fresh basil leaves, minced	

METHOD

■ Preheat the over to 350° F.

■ Cut the eggplants in half lengthwise, and scoop out most of the insides, leaving 1/2 inch of flesh all the way around,. Dice the scooped-out eggplant.

■ In a skillet, heat the olive oil. When the oil is hot, add the diced eggplant and sauté for 2 minutes over medium heat. Add the sausage, and sauté until it is cooked, about 4 to 5 minutes. Add the onion, garlic, white wine, basil, red pepper, parsley, and bread crumbs. Blend together well, and add the salt and pepper. Stir in the cheese and stuff the mixture into the eggplant shells.

■ Place the stuffed eggplant halves on a baking pan. Bake for 30 minutes or until the stuffing is golden brown on top.

Insalata Verde

GREEN SALAD

SERVES 6 TO 8

INGREDIENTS

1 medium-size head escarole	1 tablespoon red wine vinegar
1 medium-size head chicory	Salt and pepper to taste
1 medium-size head romaine lettuce	1 cup garlic croutons
1/4 cup olive oil	

METHOD

■ Break the leaves of the 3 lettuces into medium-size pieces and drop them into a chilled salad bowl. Whisk together the oil and vinegar. Pour the dressing over the greens, and toss a few times. Add salt and pepper if needed. Add the croutons, and toss again, gently, just enough to distribute the croutons evenly and to coat all the leaves with dressing.

Countryman's Salad

SERVES 4

INGREDIENTS

4 not-too-ripe Bartlett pears, peeled and quartered	4 basil leaves
	4 mint leaves
3 to 4 ounces provolone cheese, cut into sticks	Olive oil
	White pepper
1 bottle sparkling wine, divided	
1 head curly endive	

METHOD

■ Put the pears in a bowl, along with the provolone cheese and half the wine. Cover the bowl, and the let flavors blend for about 1 hour. Arrange the endive on 4 salad plates. Transfer the pears and cheese to plates and arrange on top of the endive. Dress each salad with oil, basil, mint, white pepper, and a little wine in which the pears and cheese marinated. Serve, passing the remaining half bottle of wine to drink at the table.

Insalata di Radicchio

RED CHICORY SALAD

SERVES 6

Radicchio has recently become very popular in the United States. In Italy, there are 3 different varieties of this lovely vegetable. The varieties with the long leaves have the best flavor; the variety with the cabbage-like head, most commonly found in the United States, lacks the delicate flavor of the other radicchios. Still, this is a delicious salad with any variety of radicchio, and it can be made with other greens, including dandelion greens, with excellent results.

INGREDIENTS

2 pounds radicchio	1/3 cup red wine vinegar
12 slices bacon (about 1/2 pound)	1 egg, beaten
2 garlic cloves, crushed	Salt and pepper to taste

METHOD

■ Separate the leaves of the radicchio and wash them thoroughly by immersing them in plenty of water. Drain the greens, and dry them between paper towels. Tear them coarsely into a serving bowl.

■ Cut the bacon into 1/2-inch strips and put them in a skillet with the garlic. Set the pan over moderate heat, and cook the bacon thoroughly without letting it become crisp. Remove and discard the garlic. Slowly (to avoid splattering) stir the vinegar into the bacon and the rendered fat. Let the mixture heat through to blend the flavors, and then remove the pan from heat. Let the dressing cool; then pour it over the greens. Blend in the beaten egg, and season the salad with salt and pepper. Serve immediately.

Italian Spinach Salad

SERVES 4

From the Isle of Capri

INGREDIENTS

1 pound fresh young spinach	Salt and pepper to taste
6 bacon slices	1 small garlic clove, crushed
1/4 cup olive oil	6 to 8 raw asparagus spears
1 tablespoon red wine vinegar or lemon juice	2 ounces mozzarella cheese, grated
	A few black olives

METHOD

■ Rinse the spinach by immersing it in plenty of water. Cut off the stems and spin the leaves dry.

■ Cut the bacon into small strips, put the strips in a skillet, and fry them to the desired crispness. Drain the bacon strips on paper towels, and let them cool.

■ Combine the olive oil, vinegar or lemon juice, salt and pepper, and garlic. Mix the dressing well.

■ In a salad bowl, toss the spinach with the bacon and dressing. Add the grated mozzarella cheese, olives, and asparagus spears. Toss again lightly, and serve.

Torta Pasqualina

EASTER PIE

SERVES 6

This classic is rich not only with flavor but also with meaning: the eggs symbolize fertility, the spinach symbolizes the yearly renewal of the earth, and the 33 layers of dough represent the years of Christ's life. The fillings of these tortas may vary from cook to cook, but you will find them throughout Italy at Easter time.

INGREDIENTS

8 cups all-purpose flour	Salt to taste
6 tablespoons olive oil, divided	1/4 cup butter
1 teaspoon salt	4 eggs
2 pounds fresh spinach	Freshly ground black pepper to taste
1/2 onion, minced	Pinch dried marjoram
1 pound ricotta cheese	1/4 cup grated Parmesan cheese
1 cup milk	

METHOD

▪ Mix the flour, 5 tablespoons oil, and salt, and gradually add enough water to make a stiff dough that leaves the sides of the bowl cleanly. Knead the dough. Divide it into 10 balls of equal size (originally it was divided in 33 pieces, one for each year of Christ's life). Put the balls on a lightly floured pastry board, cover them with a damp cloth, and leave them for 15 minutes.

▪ Meanwhile, wash the spinach, and cook it in as little water as possible until it is soft. Drain well.

▪ In a pan, heat 1 tablespoon olive oil. Add the onion and sauté until it is soft but not brown. Chop the spinach finely, and add it to the onion. Mix and cook the onion and the spinach for a few minutes longer, then set the pan aside.

▪ In a bowl, mix the ricotta cheese with the milk and a pinch of salt. Set the bowl aside.

▪ Preheat the oven to 400° F.

METHOD ■ Brush a deep, wide pie dish with olive oil. Roll 1 dough ball into a wafer-thin sheet a little larger in diameter than the dish; keep the rest of the balls under the damp cloth. Line the pie dish with the dough disk, brush it lightly with oil, and trim away the excess dough. Roll out another dough disk, lay it over the first, and continue layering oil and dough until 6 disks are in the pie dish. Spread the sixth disk with the onion and spinach mixture; spread the ricotta cheese over. Hollow out 6 evenly spaced wells in the filling, and drop a sliver of the butter and 1 egg into each. Sprinkle with salt, pepper, marjoram, and Parmesan cheese. Roll out the last 4 dough balls, and layer them with oil brushed between. Prick the top layer with a fork, brush it generously with oil and trim off the excess dough.

■ Bake for about 40 minutes, or until the pie is golden brown. Serve hot or cooled.

Grande Crisantemo

GRAND CHRYSANTHEMUM

SERVES 8

This dish celebrates fresh mozzarella; the original kind, made from buffalo's milk, is best. Supermarket mozzarella is no substitute.

INGREDIENTS

1/2 cup mayonnaise	5 to 6 lettuce leaves
3 tablespoons whipped cream	6 heads Belgian endive, the leaves separated
1 pound fresh mozzarella, sliced	
5 medium-size pears	1 small head radicchio
Juice of 1 lemon	1/2 cup walnut pieces

METHOD

- In a small bowl, mix the mayonnaise and cream; chill the mixture.

- Place the mozzarella in a colander to drain.

- Peel and slice 4 of the pears into wedges. Drop the wedges into a medium-size bowl, add the lemon juice, and cover the pears with water (this acidulated water will prevent the pears from discoloring).

- Line a round or oval serving dish with the lettuce. Cut the mozzarella slices into strips. In a petal-like pattern on top of the lettuce, alternate endive leaves, pear slices, and mozzarella strips; leave room in the center of the plate for a round of radicchio leaves and, in the very middle, a whole peeled pear. Arrange a second layer of endive leaves, mozzarella strips, and per slices around the whole pear, overlapping the radicchio and the first endive-pear-mozzarella layer. Continue layering the endive leaves, pear slices, and the mozzarella strips, in imitation of a chrysanthemum, until all are used.

- Sprinkle the chrysanthemum with the walnut pieces. Serve the mayonnaise-cream sauce on the side.

PIZZA & FOCACCIA

▲▲▲▲▲▲▲▲▲▲▲▲▲▲▲▲▲

When most of us Americans think of Italian food, we immediately think of pizza (or "pizza pie" as it was originally introduced in the northeastern United States). For many of us, pizza offered our first taste of Italian cooking.

The word *pizza* literally means "to flatten"; pizza is a flat leavened bread. In the Bible, in the Book of Kings, Elijah baked a "cake" on coals and survived on the strength of it for 40 days and 40 nights. The Italians called Elijah's cake *focaccia* from the Latin *focus*, meaning "hearth." Long after Elijah baked his cake, Pliny the Elder mixed "the foam of the beer" (yeast) into flour. Evidence that Romans baked risen round loaves has been found in the ruins of Pompeii and Herculaneum.

There are many different versions of focaccia in Italy, although all start with flour, salt, yeast, and water. Often fresh herbs are kneaded into the dough; some contain cheese. A favorite is Focaccia alla Genovese, which is served doused with the local olive oil. Focaccia is often served as a snack and makes a great accompaniment to soups and salads.

Pizza, as we know it today, is the invention of the Neapolitans, who began improving their circle of crust with lard, oil, herbs, and, when it was available, cheese. Not until Columbus brought the tomato to Italy from the New World was *pizza al promidoro* born—an affordable treat in the household of an Italian peasant. In the sixteenth century, the Tavern of Cerriglo in Spaccanapoli, Italy, was the first tavern anywhere to serve a tomato-and-mozzarella pizza.

The first pizzeria in America was opened in the first decade of this century, in Manhattan. It specialized in Pizza Margherita, the tomato-mozzarella-basil pizza said to have been admired by Queen Margherita because it bore the colors of the Italian flag. Pizza Margherita became known here as Pizza Neapolitan Style, and its fame soon spread throughout the country, along with Pizza Sicilian, New York Pizza, Chicago-style Pizza, and California-style Pizza.

A genuine Neapolitan pizza is very different from what is produced in most American pizza shops. It differs in the methods of baking, in the taste of the dough, and in the taste of the tomato topping.

Genuine Neapolitan pizza is baked not in a pan but on a hot brick or stone surface. Because this method lets excess oil escape, a Neapolitan pizza never tastes greasy or fried. The crust is crisp on the outside and firm throughout, faintly sour but not yeasty tasting, and never spongy or rubbery. Except for the raised edges, the crust has a uniform thickness of not more than 3/8 inch.

The tomato topping for a real Neapolitan pizza is not a sweetened sauce, but simply tomatoes; ideally, they are fully ripe so they can go into the oven raw. If you cannot find good fresh plum tomatoes, substitute the canned tomatoes from Italy.

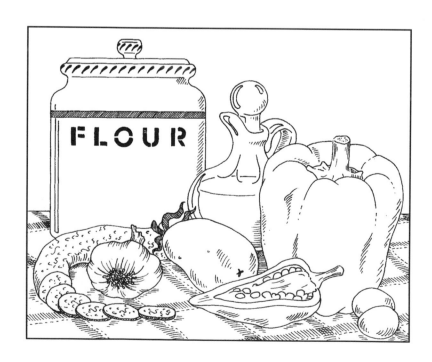

POPULAR PIZZAS

There are as many variations on the basic pizza recipe as there are bakers. Here is a listing of some of the pizza variations you may encounter at pizzerias in Italy and abroad.

Alle Cozze (*with Mussels*)

Add 1 pound shelled mussels during the last 5 to 10 minutes of cooking.

Margherita of della Regina (*of the Queen*)

Substitute fresh basil for oregano, and add sliced or diced mozzarella cheese (no garlic). This pizza is said to have been made for Queen Margherita because it bears the colors of the Italian flag—red, white, and green.

Alla Romana (*Roman-Style*)

Add anchovies (filleted or coarsely chopped) and a pinch of pepper. Finish with sliced mozzarella and a sprinkling of grated Parmesan cheese.

Alla Siciliana (*Sicilian-Style*)

Add chopped onions and anchovies. Finish with shredded caciocavallo or provolone cheese.

Alla Ligure (*Ligurian-Style*)

Season with rosemary instead of oregano and add a handful of pitted black olives.

Antica alla Frattese (*Ancient from Fratta*), or **Bianca** (*white*)

Omit the tomatoes; this pizza predates their adoption in Italy. Top the pizza with just grated cheese, oil, and a pinch of pepper. Provolone, Pecorino Romano, or caciocavallo cheese is used. Mozzarella may be added.

All'Ortolana (*Kitchen Garden-Style*)

Omit the tomatoes and substitute roasted and peeled red, yellow, and green peppers, cut into strips. Add a handful of green olives.

Alla Siracusana (*Syracuse-Style*)

Omit the fresh tomatoes. Top with fried eggplant, mozzarella slices, oregano, peppers, green olives, and a few spoonfuls of tomato sauce.

All'Amalfitana (*Amalfi-Style*)

Omit the tomatoes. Top with 1/2 pound raw small sardines (their heads removed) dressed with a mixture of olive oil, salt, pepper, and minced garlic.

Congliocchi (*with the Eyes*)

Top with tomato slices, oil, anchovies, grated Parmesan cheese, and pepper. Bake for 15 minutes. Break 4 eggs on top of the pizza and bake for 5 more minutes. Add salt and continue baking until the eggs are done, 5 to 8 minutes.

Della Luna (*of the Moon*)

Spread oil on the dough with your fingers; add nothing else. Bake for 20 minutes, then top with 1/4 cup pesto.

Quattro Stagioni (*Four Seasons*)

Score uncooked, flattened pizza dough into 4 sections with a knife. Place a different condiment in each section, as follows. First section: pitted black olives with chopped anchovies and oil. Second section: pickled artichokes in oil. Third section: sautéed mushrooms. Fourth section: raw mussels or clams tossed in olive oil (minced garlic is added during the last 5 minutes of baking). Other topping variations might be: tomato slices and diced mozzarella; prosciutto strips and diced mozzarella; chopped onions, Gruyère cheese, and ham; sautéed onions and zucchini; eggplant and oregano.

Also choose for pizza toppings: greens, fennel, cardoons, caviar, pancetta, sausage, salami, tripe, figs, chicken livers, pineapple, spaghetti, hearts of palm, tuna, snails, eels, squid, smoked salmon, smoked herring, shrimp, prawns, seaweed, oysters, asparagus, broccoli.

THE PERFECT PIZZA OVEN

In 1830, the first pizzeria appeared in Naples. It had a brick-lined oven, fired by wood. The wood was soon replaced by Vesuvian lava, which was able to retain the high temperature needed to make the best pizzas.

A conventional home oven can be transformed into something very much like a baker's oven by lining it with quarry tiles or a baking stone. The tiles or stone must be preheated for at least 30 minutes ahead of baking. If you can't find baking stones or other pizza-making equipment or ingredients locally, write to Italian foods and cooking equipment suppliers.

RISING TO THE OCCASION: ABOUT YEAST

Egyptians fermented bread dough six thousand years ago. At first the dough was thought to be spoiled and was thrown away. The Hebrews refused to eat this leavened bread. But the Egyptians learned to take advantage of the fermentation by keeping a small piece of yeasty dough as a "starter" for fresh dough. If you take the Roman *moretum* or the Tuscan *schiacciata* (both flat, unleavened circles of dough) and let it rise before baking, you have pizza as it was first made.

THROWING THE PIZZA

One final note on the mystery of pizza making concerns the debate over why the *pizzaiola* (pizza maker) throws the circle of dough into the air, sometimes executing twirls and loop-the-loops and catching it without its losing shape, folding, or tearing. Some say this is to allow more air to reach the rising dough, or to test its elasticity before adding the topping and baking it. But all agree that accomplished pizza makers enjoy doing acrobatics with the dough, as much as their customers enjoy the show.

Authentic Neapolitan Pizza Crust

MAKES 1 10- TO
11-INCH PIZZA CRUST

INGREDIENTS

1 1/2 cups semolina or hard wheat flour (substitute all-purpose flour if necessary)	**1/2 ounce fresh yeast or 1 1/2 teaspoons** (1/2 package) active dry yeast, dissolved in 1/2 cup lukewarm water
1 teaspoon salt	**1 tablespoon olive oil**

METHOD

■ Pour the flour onto a work surface, shape it into a mound, and make a shallow well in the center. Place the salt, dissolved yeast, and olive oil in the well, and draw the sides of the dough with your hands until all the ingredients are well blended and form a ball of dough. Knead the dough for about 8 minutes. (You can blend the ingredients in a food processor instead and knead by hand for 5 minutes.)

■ Put the kneaded dough in a lightly floured bowl. Fold a damp dish towel in half and lay it over the bowl. Place the bowl in a warm, draft-free place, such as an unlit oven with a gas pilot. The dough is ready to use when it has doubled in volume. if you are not ready to bake the pizza then, however, no harm will be done if you leave the dough in the bowl for an extra hour or two.

■ When the dough is ready for the toppings, set the oven at 450° F and begin heating the pizza stone or tiles. The stone or tiles should heat for at least 30 minutes.

■ Roll out the pizza dough into a disk about 10 or 11 inches in diameter and about 1/4 inch thick. Turn the dough over from time to time as you roll it to keep it from shrinking back. Try not to roll past the edges. As you reach the desired diameter, use your fingertips to push some of the dough from the center toward the edge, making the edge at least twice as thick as the rest of the crust. Place the dough on a lightly floured wooden paddle or sheet of cardboard (a light sprinkling of cornmeal also helps to prevent sticking and adds flavor to the bottom of the crust).

■ When you are ready to bake the pizza, spread the toppings evenly over the dough so the pizza will not become soggy. Slide the pizza from the paddle onto the hot stone or tiles. Bake the pizza for 15 to 20 minutes, until the edge has turned golden with a few specks of brown. Serve hot.

Sfincione

PIZZA

SERVES 6

In Palermo, street vendors and bake shops sell sfincione instead of pizza. The recipe here is for an open sfincione, which is much like a pizza. Sfincione di San Vito is closer to a pie than a pizza; its rich filling of sausage and ricotta is stuffed between two layers of bread dough.

INGREDIENTS

DOUGH

1/3 cup olive oil

Juice of 1 lemon

Salt and pepper to taste

1/4 cup grated Pecorino Romano or cacio-cavallo cheese

3 1/2 cups all-purpose flour

2/3 ounce fresh yeast or 1 tablespoon (1 package) active dry yeast dissolved in 1/2 cup warm water

TOPPING

1/3 plus 1/4 cup olive oil

1 large onion, chopped

3 to 4 tomatoes, peeled, seeded, and chopped

1/4 cup chopped fresh parsley

3/4 cup diced Pecorino Romano or cacio-cavallo cheese

6 anchovy fillets, washed and cut into pieces

2 tablespoons dry bread crumbs

METHOD

▪ To make the dough, warm 1/3 cup olive oil, and add the lemon juice, salt, pepper, and cheese. Work this mixture into the flour, then add the dissolved yeast. You should get a soft but firm dough. Knead it well.

▪ Dust a large bowl with a little flour. Add the dough. Make 2 crossed incisions in the top. Cover the dough with a cloth, and put the bowl in a warm place. Let the dough rise until it is doubled in bulk, about 2 hours.

▪ While the dough rises, prepare the topping. Heat 1/3 cup olive oil in a pan and add the onion and tomatoes. Sauté for a few minutes, then add the parsley, cheese, and 2/3 of the anchovy pieces. Cook gently over low heat for 10 to 15 minutes. Set the pan aside.

▪ When the dough has doubled in bulk, briefly knead it again. Spread it on a greased round baking pan. Let is rise for another 30 minutes in a warm place.

METHOD

■ Preheat the oven to 400° F.

■ With your finger, make indentations in the top of the dough, and spread half the topping over it. Bake the sfincione for 30 minutes. While the sfincione bakes, heat 1/4 cup olive oil with the dry bread crumbs in a frying pan. Take the sfincione out of the oven, and cover it with the rest of the topping. Garnish it with the remaining chopped anchovy, cover the top with the fried bread crumbs, and moisten with a little fresh olive oil. Bake the sfincione for another 10 minutes to bind the topping and serve.

Pizza alla Napolitana

NEAPOLITAN PIZZA

**MAKES
1 10-INCH TO
11-INCH
PIZZA**

Neapolitan pizza is topped with garlic, tomatoes, and olive oil; no cheese is added. Though today considered the most traditional pizza, this is a descendant of the older oil and garlic pizza. At its best with good tomatoes and fresh, sweet garlic, Neapolitan pizza has no rivals.

INGREDIENTS

5 tablespoons olive oil, divided	Salt
Pizza dough (see page 151)	4 medium-size garlic cloves, sliced very thin
1 1/2 pounds fresh plum tomatoes, peeled, seeded, and chopped; or 2 cups canned Italian plum tomatoes, thoroughly drained, seeded, and chopped	2 tablespoons dried oregano
	6 to 12 anchovy fillets

METHOD

■ Preheat the oven to 450° F and begin heating a pizza stone or tiles. The stone or tiles should heat for at least 30 minutes.

■ Heat 3 tablespoons of the oil in a pan. When the oil is hot, add the tomatoes. Cook them briefly over high heat, stirring, to evaporate excess moisture.

■ Roll out the dough for a 10-inch to 11-inch pizza and place it on a wooden paddle or sheet of cardboard. Top the dough with the tomatoes, a sprinkling of the salt, the garlic, the oregano, and the anchovies; then pour the remaining 2 tablespoons olive oil in a thin stream evenly over the pizza. Slide the pizza onto the hot stone or tiles, and bake for 15 to 20 minutes, until the puffed rim of the crust turns golden. Serve hot.

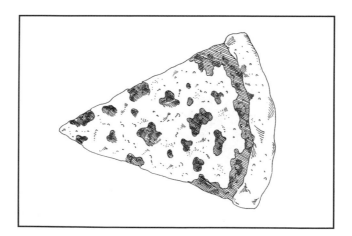

Pizza Margherita

MAKES 1 10-INCH TO 11-INCH PIZZA

This pizza, in the red, white, and green colors of the Italian flag, was made for Queen Margherita in 1889. The anchovies traditionally used in Neapolitan-style pizzas are omitted and mozzarella is added.

For Pizza alla Romana, use both mozzarella and anchovies.

INGREDIENTS

Pizza dough (page 151)	1 teaspoon salt or to taste
6 ounces whole-milk mozzarella	1 tablespoon dried oregano
5 tablespoons olive oil, divided	1 tablespoon grated Parmesan cheese
1 pound fresh ripe plum tomatoes, peeled, drained, and cut into strips	

METHOD

■ Prepare the pizza dough according to the recipe directions.

■ Unless you can find buffalo mozzarella, prepare the mozzarella cheese as follows: Shred or grate it into a bowl. Add 3 tablespoons olive oil, mix thoroughly, and let the cheese steep for at least 1 hour. Fresh buffalo mozzarella should be simply grated.

■ In a medium-size saucepan, heat the remaining 2 tablespoons olive oil. Add the tomatoes with the salt and cook. covered, for 2 to 3 minutes. When the tomatoes have softened a bit, remove the lid and cook for about 7 minutes more, stirring frequently. Transfer the tomatoes to a strainer, and let the excess liquid drain into a bowl for 5 minutes. Then mash and strain the tomatoes. Set them aside to cool.

■ Set the oven at 450° F and begin heating a pizza stone or tiles. The stone or tile should heat for at least 30 minutes.

■ Roll out the dough for a 10-inch to 11-inch pizza, and place it on a wooden paddle or sheet of cardboard. Spread the tomatoes evenly over the dough, then sprinkle on the salt, the mozzarella, the oregano, and the Parmesan cheese. Slide the pizza onto the preheated baking stone or tiles and bake for 15 to 20 minutes, until the puffed rim of the dough is golden. Serve hot.

Focaccia

SERVES 6

Like a thick pizza, focaccia has a smoother, more bread-like texture. In Puglia, this would be called a *puddica*.

INGREDIENTS

Pinch salt	2/3 ounce fresh yeast or 1 tablespoon
4 1/2 cups all-purpose flour	(1 package) active dry yeast, dissolved
	in 1/2 cup warm water

METHOD

■ Mix the salt with the flour; add the dissolved yeast and about 1 1/2 cups more water to make a soft but firm dough. Knead until the dough is smooth and elastic. Let it rise for at least 30 minutes, until it has doubled in bulk.

■ Preheat the oven to 400° F. Roll out the dough at least 1 1/2 inches thick, and place in greased pan. Bake for 30 to 45 minutes, until golden. Let it cool before cutting and serving. It is very good with cheese, ham, salami, and so on.

VARIATION

Add to the dough or top the dough with any one or more of the following: rosemary, sage, garlic, tomatoes, cheeses, sausage, onions, ciccioli (cracklings), hard-boiled eggs, or prosciutto. You can also substitute white wine for water in the dough, Puglian style.

DESSERTS & SWEETS

▲▲▲▲▲▲▲▲▲▲▲▲▲▲▲▲▲▲

Few travelers return from Italy without rapturous reports of the pastries and gelato they consumed there. They talk of afternoons spent at cafes, drinking espresso, and eating the most wonderful almond-filled, lemon-scented, rum-flavored, chocolate-coated pastries. They speak of cannoli, biscotti, crespelles, and torta.

Gelato is sold by vendors on street corners throughout Europe, and even in some favored areas of the United States. Italian pastries can be found in bakeries and cafes throughout the world. If you are lucky enough to be invited to an Italian wedding, you will have an opportunity to sample a wide range of the best Italian sweets. Italian wedding cake is like none other. Sinfully rich, moist, spongy cake is layered with pastry creme and laced with fruit preserves and liqueur, then topped with roses made from melt-in-your-mouth frosting. Here is a listing of some of the many sweets you are likely to encounter on your culinary travels through Italy.

PASTRIES

Baba Rum. Rum-soaked sponge-cake filled with pastry cream and a dab of fruit.

Cannoli alla Siciliana. Sicilian fried pastry tubes filled with sweetened ricotta cheese.

Pasticca. Small sweet-dough pies filled with vanilla or chocolate cream, with rum-soaked bottoms.

Spolietelle. Special occasion torte.

ICES AND ICE CREAM

Gelato. Flavored ice cream.

Granita. A frozen slush of fruit juice or coffee and sugar.

Spumoni. Ice cream bombe (many flavors, colors, textures).

Tortoni. Rum-flavored ice cream macaroon treat served in paper cups.

OTHER DESSERTS

Biscotti all'Anise, Anisette. Anisette-flavored biscuit, good for dipping.

Budino di Ricotta. Ricotta pudding.

Cassata Gelata. Ice cream cake.

Cassata di Ricotta. Ricotta cheesecake.

Ciambella Milanese alla Caffe. Milanese coffeecake.

Crespelle. Italian crepes, served warm with orange sauce.

Fiche Ripieni. Stuffed figs.

Panettone. Fruit-bread, a Christmas special.

Pan di Spagna. Sponge cake.

Struffoli alla Napoletana. Neapolitan honey-balls.

Tartine alla Crema. Little cream tarts.

Torta alla Zabaglione. Custard cake with Marsala wine.

Torta di Mele alla Mantova. Apple cake, Mantua-style.

Zabaglione. Custard with Marsala wine.

Zuccotto. Fancy, dome-shaped, layered dessert with sponge cake, liqueur-laced chocolate, and fruit fillings.

Zuppa Inglese. Italian trifle.

Gelato alla Vaniglia

VANILLA ICE CREAM

MAKES 2 QUARTS

It is not necessary to have an ice cream maker to produce this wonderful treat.

INGREDIENTS

6 egg yolks	1 cup sugar
2 cups whole milk	1 teaspoon vanilla extract
2 cups whipping cream	

METHOD

- Beat the egg yolks until foamy.

- Combine the milk, cream, and sugar in the top of a double boiler. Heat the mixture until small bubbles form around the side of the pan. Add a small amount of the cream mixture to the egg yolks, then stir the yolks into the cream in the top of the double boiler. Cook the custard over simmering water, stirring constantly, until it thickens enough to lightly coat a metal spoon. Stir in the vanilla. Strain the custard; let it cool thoroughly.

- Freeze the custard in an ice cream maker according to the manufacturer's directions. If you have no ice cream maker, proceed as follows.

- Pour the custard into two deep metal freezer trays and cover the trays with foil. Freeze the custard until it is firm, but not hard.

- Chill the bowl and beater of an electric mixer. Empty the freezer trays into the mixing bowl; beat the custard at high speed until it has doubled in volume. Return it to the trays and freeze until it is firm, but not hard.

- Break up the custard, beat it again, and freeze it until it is firm but not hard.

- Beat the frozen custard a third time, then put it into a bowl and cover it. Freeze the gelato until it is firm again, about 2 hours.

- Store the gelato in the freezer until you are ready to serve it.

159

Gelato al Caffe

COFFEE ICE CREAM

**MAKES 1
QUART**

This is a very simple recipe; if you have an ice cream maker, it takes only 35 minutes to prepare.

INGREDIENTS

1/3 cup instant coffee powder	1/2 cup sugar
1 1/4 cups milk, heated	3/4 cup whipping cream
6 egg yolks	

METHOD

▪ Add the instant coffee to the hot milk, and stir until the coffee dissolves.

▪ In a bowl, beat the yolks and sugar. Stir in hot coffee mixture and blend thoroughly. Let the mixture cool to room temperature, about 20 minutes; then stir in cream. Taste to see if it is sweet enough. If not add more sugar.

▪ Freeze the mixture in an ice cream maker according to the manufacturer's directions, or in a freezer tray, beating the mixture several times as it freezes (see preceding recipe).

▪ Store the gelato in the freezer until you are ready to serve it.

Granita di Limone

LEMON ICE

SERVES 4

INGREDIENTS

1 cup sugar	1 cup lemon juice
	1 tablespoon lemon zest

METHOD

▪ Combine the sugar and 2 cups water in a saucepan. Boil gently for 5 minutes. Cool to room temperature, then stir in the lemon juice and zest.

▪ Freeze the granita in an ice cream maker according to the manufacturer's directions, or in a freezer tray, beating the mixture several times as it freezes.

▪ Store the granita in the freezer until you are ready to serve it.

Zabaglione

CUSTARD WITH MARSALA WINE

**SERVES
1 TO 2**

According to legend, this famous sweet was invented by accident, when the chef to Carlo Emanuele I of Savoy accidentally added some fortified sweet wine to an egg custard. An immediate success, the dish was dedicated to the patron saint of pastry makers, San Giovanni Baylon, hence the name. Zabaglione is said to have great restorative powers, and it is customarily served to newlyweds as an aphrodisiac.

INGREDIENTS

3 yolks of large eggs (or 4 yolks of medium-size eggs)

3 tablespoons sugar

1 cup dry Marsala wine

METHOD

■ Heat water in the bottom of a double boiler.

■ Place the egg yolks in a bowl and add the sugar. Stir with a wooden spoon, always in the same direction, until the sugar is completely dissolved and the mixture lightens in color. Add the Marsala slowly, then transfer the egg mixture to the top of the double boiler. Heat over boiling water, stirring constantly, and always in the same direction, until the mixture thickens and sticks to the wooden spoon (4 to 5 minutes). Do not allow to boil. When the mixture has thickened, remove the top pan of the double boiler, and keep stirring for another 2 to 3 minutes to cool the zabaglione. Cover the zabaglione with lightly buttered waxed paper, and let it cool for 1 hour at room temperature; then refrigerate until you are ready to serve it in goblets or cups.

VARIATION I

For a creamier zabaglione, whip 1 cup whipping cream with 2 tablespoons sugar and fold into the cooled custard.

VARIATION II

Place strawberry halves or blueberries in the bottom of the goblets prior to pouring in the zabaglione.

Spuma di Cioccolata

CHOCOLATE MOUSSE

SERVES 6

INGREDIENTS

8 ounces semisweet chocolate, cut into small pieces

3 eggs

1 cup whipping cream

1/4 cup orange-flavored liqueur or rum (optional)

Whipped cream

Grated semisweet chocolate

METHOD

■ Melt the chocolate over very low heat or in a microwave. Set aside to cool slightly.

■ Beat the eggs in a medium-size bowl until they are foamy. Set aside.

■ Beat the eggs gradually into the cooled chocolate. Blend in the orange liqueur or rum, if desired; do not overbeat the mixture. Beat the whipping cream in a large bowl until stiff peaks form. Fold the chocolate mixture into the whipped cream until thoroughly combined.

■ Spoon the mousse into individual dessert glasses, and decorate with whipped cream and grated chocolate. Refrigerate the glasses overnight. Serve the mousse chilled.

Cassata all'Italiana

ITALIAN DESSERT

SERVES 8

Donatello's scrumptious frozen version of the famous Italian cake.

INGREDIENTS

1/3 cup raisins	1/2 cup sliced toasted hazelnuts
1/2 cup dry Marsala wine	3 tablespoons blanched pistachios, chopped
1/2 cup sugar	1 pound fresh strawberries, hulled
2 egg whites	Sugar
3/4 cup whipping cream, whipped	Mint sprigs
1/2 cup mixed diced candied fruit	

METHOD

■ In a small bowl, soak the raisins in the Marsala for 1 hour. Drain well and set aside.

■ Heat the sugar with 1/2 cup water in a small, heavy saucepan over low heat, swirling the pan occasionally, until the sugar dissolves. Increase the heat and boil the syrup until a candy thermometer reads 234° F to 240° F (the soft-ball stage).

■ While the syrup boils, beat the egg whites in an electric mixer until soft peaks form. Slowly pour the hot syrup down the side of the mixer bowl, and beat until the syrup is incorporated and the whites are thick and cool. Gently fold in the whipped cream, candied fruit, hazelnuts, pistachios, and raisins. Spoon the mixture into a 9-inch by 5-inch loaf pan, pressing down to eliminate air bubbles. Smooth the top, cover the cassata with plastic wrap, and freeze for at least 3 hours.

■ Purée the strawberries in a food processor or blender; strain out the seeds. Add sugar to taste. Run a sharp knife around the cassata. Wrap a hot towel around the pan, and invert the cassata onto a platter. To serve, spoon the strawberry sauce onto plates, and top with slices of cassata. Garnish with mint.

Blueberry Tortoni

SERVES 8

Cousin Anna acquired this recipe years ago from Mamma Leone's famous Italian restaurant near the Broadway theaters in Manhattan.

INGREDIENTS

1/2 cup sugar	1 1/2 cups whipping cream, whipped
3 egg yolks	1 cup fresh blueberries or 1 cup frozen unsweetened blueberries
2/3 cup almond paste	Grated almonds
3 tablespoons pineapple juice or light cream	
Dash salt	

METHOD

■ Combine the sugar and 1/4 cup water in a saucepan, and bring the mixture to a boil. Boil until a candy thermometer registers 240° F.

■ While the syrup boils, beat the egg yolks until they are thick and lemon colored. Gradually beat the hot syrup into the yolks; continue beating until the mixture is very thick. Gradually beat in the almond paste, pineapple juice, and salt. Fold in the whipped cream, then the blueberries.

■ Spoon the mixture into 4-ounce soufflé cups. Decorate the top of each serving with a few blueberries and grated almonds. Place the cups in the freeze, and freeze until the tortoni are firm. When they are frozen hard, wrap them in plastic freezer wrap to prevent crystallizing. Serve frozen.

Semifreddo di Torrone

SEMIFROZEN TORRONE CANDIES

SERVES 8

Semifrozen desserts are enjoying a great popularity in American restaurants. Torrone, which forms the basis for this dish, is a fancy nougat candy. It is sold in both hard and soft varieties in Italian markets, some supermarkets, and specialty stores.

INGREDIENTS

3 eggs, separated, at room temperature

1/2 cup sugar

2 3/4 cups whipping cream

2 tablespoons dark rum

1 tablespoon vanilla extract

4 ounces bittersweet chocolate, finely chopped

3 ounces hard torrone, crushed into rice-size pieces

1 1/2 tablespoons powdered sugar

4 teaspoons unsweetened cocoa powder

Chocolate curls

METHOD

■ Line a 5-inch by 10-inch loaf pan with plastic wrap, allowing the edges to overhang.

■ Whisk the egg yolks and sugar in a bowl until it is thick and pale yellow.

■ Beat 1 1/4 cups of the cream until soft peaks form.

■ Beat the egg whites until they are stiff but not dry.

■ Fold the whipped cream, egg whites, rum, and vanilla into the yolk mixture.

■ Combine the chopped chocolate and torrone in a small bowl. Sprinkle 1/3 of this mixture into the prepared pan. Top with 1/3 of the cream mixture, pressing firmly. Repeat this process 2 more times with the remaining chocolate mixture and the cream. Fold the plastic wrap over the top of the pan, and freeze the dessert for at least 3 hours and up to 1 week.

■ Unmold the dessert onto a platter. Let it soften for 30 minutes in the refrigerator.

■ Sift together the powdered sugar and cocoa. Beat the remaining 1 1/2 cups cream until soft peaks form, and fold the cream into the cocoa mixture. Beat the cocoa cream until stiff peaks form.

■ Spread a thin layer of the cocoa cream over the dessert, covering it completely. Spoon the remaining cream into a pastry bag fitted with a large star tip. Pipe the cream decoratively along the edges and around the base of the dessert. Garnish with chocolate curls and serve.

Pere Cotte con Creme e Cioccolato

PEARS STUFFED WITH CHOCOLATE AND WHIPPED CREAM

SERVES 12

INGREDIENTS

12 ripe bosc pears	2 cups sugar
2/3 cup lemon juice	1 1/3 cups orange juice
6 cups white wine	Whipped cream
Zest of 1/2 lemon	Chopped nuts
4 whole cloves	Hot chocolate sauce

METHOD

■ Peel each pear, but leave the stem attached. Slice off the bottom of the pear so it will stand up straight. Remove the core and line the hollow with aluminum foil. Stand the pears upright in a saucepan. Pour in the lemon juice, white wine, and enough water to cover the fruit. Add the lemon zest, cloves, sugar, and orange juice. Simmer, covered, for about 20 minutes, or until the pears are tender.

■ Remove the pears from the saucepan and place them on a serving dish. Cover them with foil and set aside to cool.

■ Remove the lemon zest and cloves from the syrup, and cook the syrup over low heat for about 1 1/2 hours to reduce it. Let the syrup cool.

■ After the pears have cooled, remove their foil lining. Lay each pear on a small serving dish. Fold the chopped nuts into the whipped cream, and gently spoon the mixture into the hollow of each pear. Pour a little syrup over the pear, and decorate it with the hot chocolate sauce. Serve.

Fiche Ripiene

STUFFED FIGS

SERVES 4

Stuffed figs are very popular all over Italy. But this recipe is less common; here figs are stuffed with cheese and almond filling.

INGREDIENTS

4 ripe even-sized figs	1 cup ricotta cheese
Yolk of 1 large egg	1 to 2 tablespoons brandy
1/4 cup sugar	4 shelled whole almonds

METHOD

■ Cut each half fig lengthwise down the middle, but don't separate the pieces completely. Open out each fig in quarters, and place it on a serving plate.

■ In a bowl, combine the egg yolk, sugar, and cheese; beat together until the mixture is light. Add the brandy, and fold it lightly into the cheese mixture. Spoon the mixture into the center of each fig, and top with an almond.

Fiche all Cioccolato

STUFFED FIGS IN CHOCOLATE

MAKES 1 1/2 POUNDS

INGREDIENTS

1 pound large dried figs	1/2 teaspoon ground cloves
1 cup toasted almonds	3/4 cup unsweetened cocoa
3/4 cup diced candied citrus peel	3/4 cup powdered sugar

METHOD

■ Preheat the oven to 350° F. Cut the figs lengthwise, not all the way through. Stuff each fig with an almond, a few pieces of candied peel, and a pinch of clove. Gently press the fig shut. Arrange the stuffed figs on a baking sheet. Bake for 15 minutes, or until the figs darken slightly.

■ While the figs bake, sift the cocoa and sugar together into a shallow dish. Remove the figs from the oven, let them cool enough to handle, and roll them in the cocoa mixture. Serve them when they have cooled completely, or store them in an airtight container.

Cerino's Ricotta Cheesecake

MAKES 1 10-INCH CHEESECAKE

INGREDIENTS

1 pound ricotta cheese	3 tablespoons cornstarch
1 pound cream cheese	3 tablespoons lemon juice
2 cups sour cream	1 teaspoon vanilla extract
1 1/2 cups sugar	1/2 cup melted butter
4 eggs	Graham cracker crumbs
3 tablespoons all-purpose flour	

METHOD

■ Mix together the cheeses, sour cream, and sugar. Add the eggs, 1 at a time; do not overmix. Stir in the flour, cornstarch, lemon juice, and vanilla extract. Fold in the melted butter.

■ Butter a 10-inch springform baking pan and dust it well with graham cracker crumbs to form the crust. Pour in the cheese mixture. Place the cheesecake in a cold oven, then set the temperature at 325° F. Bake for 1 hour, then turn off the oven. Remove the cake from the oven 2 hours later, and remove the side of the springform pan. Slide the cake off the bottom of the springform pan and onto a plate. Serve cooled.

Castagnioli

FRIED DOUGH

SERVES 8 TO 10

INGREDIENTS

2 teaspoons vegetable oil	1 tablespoon sugar
6 eggs	About 2 1/2 cups all-purpose flour
3 tablespoons whiskey or rum	Vegetable oil for frying
Zest of 1 lemon	

METHOD

■ Beat the oil with the eggs until light. Add the rest of ingredients, using just enough flour to hold the dough together. Heat enough oil in a frying pan to deep-fry the castagnioli. Drop in large spoonfuls of the dough. Fry them until they are golden brown. Remove them with a slotted spoon and drain on paper towels. Serve them with honey.

Sicilian Cassata

SERVES 6

This is a homespun version of a most famous Sicilian sweet.

INGREDIENTS

1 1/2 pounds very fresh ricotta cheese	3 1/2 ounces unsweetened chocolate, finely chopped
2/3 to 1 cup sugar	
7 tablespoons rum	1 pound sponge cake, sliced, or ladyfingers
10 ounces candied lemon peel	

METHOD

■ Using a large bowl and a wooden spoon, cream the ricotta until it is very smooth. Add the sugar, 1 tablespoon of rum, the peel, and the chocolate.

■ Sprinkle 5 tablespoons of the rum over the sponge cake slices.

■ Line the bottom and side of a springform pan or soufflé dish with parchment paper, and brush the paper with the remaining 1 tablespoon rum. Then line the bottom and side of the pan with sponge cake slices. Fill the middle with the ricotta mixture. Refrigerate the cassata for at least 3 hours, and serve.

169

Italian Rum Cake

SERVES 8

INGREDIENTS

CAKE

6 eggs, at room temperature

1 cup sugar

1 cup self-rising flour

1/2 cup unsalted butter or margarine, melted and cooled

1 teaspoon vanilla extract

1/4 cup rum

RUM BUTTER FROSTING

1/2 cup butter, softened

1 pound powdered sugar, sifted

1 egg, well beaten

1 teaspoon vanilla extract

2 tablespoons dark rum

METHOD

■ Preheat the oven to 350° F.

■ With an electric mixer, beat the eggs at high speed until they are thick and lemon-colored. With the beater still running at high speed, add the sugar gradually, 1 tablespoon at a time. When you have added all the sugar, beat the mixture for 10 minutes, or until it has tripled in volume. Gradually, fold in the flour with a wooden spoon. (Self-rising flour makes for a smooth, fine-grained cake that is easy to handle.) Pour the melted butter slowly into the batter, leaving the milky residue behind in the pan. Fold the butter into the batter. Fold in the vanilla extract.

■ Grease the bottoms (only) of two 9-inch layer-cake pans. Line the bottoms with foil, and grease the foil. Pour the batter into the pans, and spread it evenly. Bake the cake for 25 to 30 minutes, or until it feels springy to the touch. Cool the cake in the pans for 10 minutes. With a sharp knife, cut the sides of the cake away from the pan. Remove the cake from the pans, remove the foil, and let the cake cool on racks. Sprinkle each layer with rum.

■ To make the frosting, cream the butter until it is soft and fluffy. Gradually beat in some of the sugar. Beat in the egg, vanilla, and rum. Beat in the remaining sugar gradually, until the frosting has a good spreading consistency.

■ When the cake has cooled completely, spread frosting over 1 layer, and put the second layer on top. Spread frosting over the second layer, then over the side of the cake. Refrigerate the cake to harden the frosting; this makes it easier to cut neat, thin slices.

Ricotta Rice Pie

MAKES 3
(10-INCH)
PIES

The recipe for this traditional Easter treat was passed on to Cousin Marie from her mother-in-law years ago. Marie and her sisters, Anna and Frances, are great Italian-American cooks.

INGREDIENTS

CRUST

3 tablespoons butter	
4 cups all-purpose flour	
1 cup sugar	
4 teaspoons baking powder	
4 eggs	
4 teaspoons vanilla extract	
1 teaspoon lemon extract, orange extract, or orange juice	

FILLING

1 dozen eggs	
2 cups plus 2 tablespoons sugar	
1 quart milk, warmed	
Juice and grated zest of 1 orange	
Juice and grated zest of 1/2 lemon	
2 pounds ricotta cheese	
2 cups cooked white rice	
Nutmeg (optional)	

METHOD

■ Cut the butter into the flour with a fork or pastry blender. Blend in the sugar and baking powder. Beat the eggs, one at a time, and add them to the flour mixture, mixing after each egg is incorporated. Mix in the extracts. Form the dough into a ball. Knead in a little water or orange juice if necessary. Divide the dough into thirds. Form each piece into a ball; roll out each ball on a floured surface. Lay the dough in three 10-inch pie pans; trim away the excess and pinch the edges.

■ Preheat the oven to 350° F.

■ For the filling, beat 6 egg whites with 2 tablespoons sugar until the whites are stiff. Set them aside.

■ Beat 6 whole eggs with the remaining 6 yolks and 2 cups sugar. Add the orange juice and zest and the lemon juice and zest to the warm milk. Add the milk and juice mixture to the whole egg and sugar mixture. Stir in the ricotta cheese and cooked rice. Beat all the ingredients together, then fold in the egg whites until the mixture is smooth. Dust the crust with a little flour, then pour in the filling. Sprinkle the pie with nutmeg, if you like.

■ Put aluminum foil around the edge of each pie and place the pies in the oven. Bake for about 1 hour, or until the filling has set. Check the pies after 45 minutes; if they are brown, reduce the heat to 300° F and continue baking. Serve warm or cooled.

Sfinge di San Guiseppe

ST. JOSEPH'S CREAM PUFFS

SERVES 8

INGREDIENTS

FILLING

1 cup ricotta cheese
2 tablespoons chopped semisweet chocolate
1 teaspoon grated orange zest
1/3 cup powdered sugar
1/2 cup whipping cream, whipped
1 teaspoon almond extract

PUFFS

1/2 cup butter or margarine
1 cup all-purpose flour
1/4 teaspoon salt
4 eggs
1 teaspoon grated orange zest
8 maraschino cherries
Candied orange peel

METHOD

■ For the filling, combine the ricotta cheese, chocolate, orange zest, and powdered sugar. Blend well. Fold in the whipped cream and almond extract. Chill well.

■ Preheat the oven to 375° F.

■ For the puffs, combine 1 cup water and the butter in a deep saucepan. Bring to a boil and cook until the butter melts. Quickly stir in the flour and salt. Beat until the dough forms a ball in the center of the pan. Remove the pan from the heat and let it stand for 5 minutes. Add the eggs 1 at a time, beating thoroughly after each addition. Beat in the orange zest. The mixture should be very stiff.

■ Drop spoonfuls of the mixture onto a buttered baking sheet. Bake the puffs for 20 minutes, or until they are firm and crusty. Prick them with a fork to release steam, and leave them in the oven for another 5 minutes. Remove them from the oven and let them cool.

■ Cut off the tops of the puffs, and fill them with the cheese filling. Decorate them with maraschino cherries and strips of candied orange peel, and serve.

Crema Pasticcera

PASTRY CREAM

MAKES 2 CUPS

This custard forms the basis of many Italian desserts.

INGREDIENTS

4 tablespoons sugar, divided	2 teaspoons cornstarch
1 1/3 cups light cream	1/8 teaspoon salt
2 egg yolks	1/4 teaspoon vanilla extract
2 whole eggs	1/4 teaspoon finely grated lemon zest

METHOD

■ In a saucepan over low heat, dissolve 2 tablespoons of the sugar in the cream. Scold the mixture, but don't let it boil.

■ In a mixing bowl, beat together the egg yolks, whole eggs, cornstarch, salt, and the remaining 2 tablespoons sugar. Vigorously beat in the scalded cream, and heat the mixture (without letting it boil) for a few minutes, until the cream thickens. Remove the pan from the heat and stir in the vanilla extract and lemon zest. Let the mixture cool, then chill it. Crema Pasticcera may be kept under refrigeration for 2 to 3 days; do not freeze it.

VARIATIONS

For Chocolate Crema Pasticcera, mix 2 to 4 ounces grated semisweet chocolate into the cream as you heat it. For Almond Crema Pasticcera, substitute almond extract for the vanilla extract.

Pasta Folle

FILLED PASTRY

SERVES 6

A traditional Venetian dessert.

INGREDIENTS

PASTRY

1/2 cup butter

2 2/3 cups all-purpose flour

3 eggs

2 egg yolks

1 teaspoon vanilla extract

Zest of 1 orange

FILLING

1/4 pound spinach, finely chopped

1/2 cup plus 2 tablespoons ricotta cheese

4 eggs

1/2 cup plus 2 tablespoons sugar

Juice of 1 orange

1/4 cup rum

TOPPING

3 egg whites

1 cup powdered sugar

1 cup chopped almonds

Juice of 1 lemon

METHOD

■ To make the pastry, cut the butter into the flour. Slowly stir in the eggs, one at a time, then the yolks, mixing thoroughly. Stir in the vanilla extract and orange rind. On a lightly floured surface, knead the dough briefly until it becomes a smooth mass. Roll out the dough, and line a 9-inch cake pan with it. Trim away the excess dough.

■ Preheat the oven to 350° F.

■ To make the filling, cook the spinach and drain it thoroughly. Mix it with the ricotta cheese.

■ In a separate bowl, beat the eggs with the sugar until light and lemon-colored. Add the orange juice and rum. Combine this mixture with the spinach and ricotta cheese.

■ To make the topping, beat the egg whites until they are stiff but not dry. Slowly beat in the powdered sugar, 1 tablespoon at a time. Fold in the chopped nuts and lemon juice.

■ Spread the filling in the pastry-lined pan. Spread the topping over the filling. Place the pie in the hot oven and bake for about 40 minutes. Serve hot.

Cannoli alla Siciliana

SICILIAN PASTRY TUBES

MAKES 10
PASTRIES

These Sicilian sweets are readily available in bakeries throughout the United States. They are fried pastry tubes filled with sweetened ricotta.

INGREDIENTS

FILLING

1 1/2 cups ricotta cheese

1/4 cup chopped candied fruit

3 tablespoons chopped pistachio nuts or almonds

2 to 3 tablespoons chopped semisweet chocolate

3 tablespoons sugar

1/4 teaspoon almond extract

PASTRY

1 cup all-purpose flour, sifted

2/3 cup sugar

1/4 teaspoon salt

1/4 cup Marsala wine

Vegetable oil

Powdered sugar

METHOD

■ Combine the ricotta cheese, candied fruit, nuts, 2 tablespoons of the chocolate, the sugar, and almond extract. Mix well. Chill. To make the pastry, sift together the flour, sugar, and salt. Stir in the wine. Knead the dough on a floured surface until it is firm and elastic. Add another drop or two of wine, if necessary, but do not allow the dough to become sticky. Place the dough in a lightly floured bowl, cover the bowl with a damp towel, and let it stand for 2 hours.

■ Roll out the dough on a lightly floured surface to a rectangle 22 1/2 inches by 9 inches; the dough should be 1/8 inch thick. Cut the dough into ten 4 1/2-inch squares. Wrap each square diagonally around a cannoli tube or a clean, unpainted piece of broomstick 6 inches long. Moisten the points that will overlap with a drop of water, and press firmly to seal.

■ In a large, deep pan, heat vegetable oil to deep-fry the cannoli. Fry them, 3 or 4 at a time, until they are golden brown. Drain them on paper towels for about 30 seconds. Using tongs, carefully slide the forms out of the cannoli. Let the cannoli cool.

■ Just before serving, fill the cannoli with the chilled ricotta mixture. If you like, garnish the ends with more chocolate, and dust the cannoli tubes with powdered sugar.

Bocconotti

LITTLE MOUTHFULS

MAKES 2 TO 4 DOZEN TARTS

Jam or custard-filled pastries from Naples.

INGREDIENTS

4 cups all-purpose flour

3 tablespoons sugar

2 to 3 tablespoons vegetable oil

Blackberry or quince jam, or plain or chocolate Crema Pasticcera (pastry, cream, page 173)

1 egg yolk, beaten

METHOD

■ Preheat the oven to 425° F.

■ Combine the flour and sugar. Mix in the oil and enough water to make a soft dough. On a floured work surface, roll the pastry out thin, and cut out disks 2 or 3 inches in diameter. Place a dab of jam or Crema Pasticcera in the center of each disk. Fold the disk in half, and press the edges firmly together to seal them. Lay the bocconotti on a baking pan, and brush with the egg yolk.

■ Bake for about 20 minutes; check after 15 minutes, and every 5 minutes thereafter. When done, they will be golden brown. Serve cooled.

Nepitelle

LITTLE TARTS

MAKES 24 TARTS

These delectable little tarts are filled with dried fruit and grated chocolate.

INGREDIENTS

MARSALA PASTRY

2 cups all-purpose flour

1/4 cup sugar

Pinch salt

1/2 cup plus 1 tablespoon butter, well-chilled

3 tablespoons sweet Marsala wine

2 teaspoons grated lemon zest

1 egg, beaten

FRUIT FILLING

1/4 cup sweet Marsala wine

1/2 cup raisins

1/3 cup minced dried figs (about 1 1/2 ounces)

3 tablespoons sugar

1 1/2 ounces bittersweet chocolate, grated

1/4 teaspoon ground cinnamon

Pinch salt

METHOD

■ To make the pastry, sift the flour, sugar, and salt into a large bowl. Cut in the butter until the mixture resembles coarse meal. Make a well in the center. Add the Marsala, lemon zest, and egg to the well and mix these ingredients with a fork until they are well blended.

■ Continue mixing, gradually drawing the flour from the inner edge of the well, until all the flour is incorporated. Gather the dough into a ball and wrap it in plastic film. Chill for at least 30 minutes, and up to 2 days.

■ Butter twenty-four 2-inch tartlet pans. Roll the dough out on a lightly floured surface to a thickness of 1/16 inch. Using a floured cutter or drinking glass, cut out 3-inch-diameter rounds. Fit the rounds into the prepared pans, trim the edges, and refrigerate the pastry shells.

■ To make the filling, heat the Marsala in a small heavy saucepan. Remove the pan from the heat, add the raisins, and leave them to plump for about 30 minutes. Stir in the figs, sugar, chocolate, cinnamon, and salt. (The fillings can be prepared up to 1 week ahead and refrigerated.)

■ Preheat the over to 400° F.

■ Spoon 1 tablespoon of the filling into each pastry shell. Bake until the pastry is lightly browned, 15 to 20 minutes. Cool the tartlets on a rack, then remove them from their pans. Sprinkle them with powdered sugar. Serve the tartlets immediately, or store them at room temperature for up to 1 day.

Struffoli

SERVES 8

These traditional honey-coated Christmas sweets are often piled into a pyramid as a centerpiece for the holiday table; the struffoli are broken off and eaten at the end of the meal.

INGREDIENTS

2 1/4 cups all-purpose flour, sifted	1/2 teaspoon vanilla extract
3 tablespoons grated orange zest	Vegetable oil
1 tablespoon grated lemon zest	3/4 cup honey
1/4 teaspoon salt	1 tablespoon sugar
3 tablespoons butter, at room temperature	1 cup mixed candied fruit
3 eggs, at room temperature, beaten	Additional candied fruit (optional)

METHOD

■ Combine the flour, 1 tablespoon of the orange zest, the lemon zest, and the salt on a work surface. Cut in the butter. Mound the mixture and make a well in the center. Add the eggs and vanilla to the well. Mixing with a fork, gradually draw the flour mixture from the inner edge of the well into the center. Mix until the flour is completely incorporated. Knead the dough until it is smooth, about 5 minutes, adding more flour if necessary to prevent sticking. Cover the dough loosely. Let it stand for 1 hour at room temperature.

■ Break off walnut-size pieces of the dough. With your palms, roll each piece out on a work surface to a pencil-thin strip 14 to 15 inches long. Cut each dough strip into 1/4-inch pieces.

■ Heat vegetable oil to deep-fry the struffoli. Gently place a few pieces of the dough in the hot oil; do not crowd them. Fry the struffoli, a few at a time, until they are golden brown, 45 to 60 seconds. Remove them with a slotted spoon and drain them on paper towels.

■ Butter a large plate. Heat the honey and sugar in a large, heavy saucepan over medium heat until the mixture is clear, about 5 minutes. Add the remaining 2 tablespoons orange zest, the struffoli and the candied fruit. Transfer the honey-coated struffoli and candied fruit to the buttered plate, and let them cool slightly, 5 to 7 minutes. Moisten your hands with cold water and shape the struffoli into a pyramid. Decorate the pyramid with additional candied fruit, if desired. The struffoli will keep for 1 day; cover and store the pyramid at room temperature if it is not to be eaten within a few hours.

Germinus

SARDINIAN MACAROONS

MAKES ABOUT 1 POUND

INGREDIENTS

4 egg whites	3/4 pound peeled and slivered almonds
3/4 pound powdered sugar	Juice of 1 lemon

METHOD

■ Preheat the oven to 325° F.

■ Beat the egg whites until stiff peaks form. Fold in the sugar together with the almonds and lemon juice. Cover a baking pan with parchment paper, and place spoonfuls of the mixture on it, spaced well apart.

■ Bake for about 25 minutes, or until the macaroons are lightly colored. Allow them to cool before removing them from the parchment paper. Serve the cookies immediately, or store them in an airtight container.

Biscotti

COOKIES

MAKES 4 DOZEN SMALL COOKIES

INGREDIENTS

2 egg yolks	1/4 teaspoon grated orange zest
1/2 teaspoon vanilla extract	1 egg, beaten
2 1/4 cups all-purpose flour	Decoration: Maraschino cherries, pine nuts, cinnamon sugar, ginger sugar, plain coarse sugar, sliced candied fruit, or chopped nuts (almonds, cashews, pecans, pistachios, or walnuts)
3/4 cup sugar	
1/4 teaspoon salt	
1/4 cup butter, cut into bits	

METHOD

■ Beat together the egg yolks and vanilla extract.

■ Sift together the flour, sugar, and salt onto a pastry board or into a bowl. Make a well in the center of the mound, and place in it the butter, orange zest, and combined egg yolks and vanilla. With your fingers, quickly work these ingredients into the flour to produce a thick, smooth dough. Shape the dough into a ball, wrap it in waxed paper, and chill it for 30 minutes.

■ Preheat the oven to 350° F.

■ Roll the dough to a thickness of 1/4 inch and cut out rounds about 2 1/2 inches in diameter. Brush them with the beaten egg and decorate them with one of the suggested decorations listed above.

■ Arrange the cookies on a cookie sheet. Bake for 12 minutes, or until they are lightly browned. Remove them to a rack to cool

VARIATIONS

For Chocolate Biscotti. blend 1 1/2 ounces semisweet chocolate, melted and cooled, into the dough before cutting it. For Almond Biscotti, substitute almond extract for the vanilla extract.

Biscotti al'Anici

ANISE COOKIES

MAKES 24 TO 42 SMALL COOKIES

INGREDIENTS

1 cup sugar	2 1/2 teaspoons baking powder
1 cup butter	6 to 8 drops anise oil, or 3 to 4 drops anise oil and 3 to 4 drops vanilla extract
3 eggs	
3 cups all-purpose flour	

METHOD

■ Preheat the oven to 375° F. Grease two 9-inch by 5-inch loaf pans.

■ In a large bowl, cream together the sugar and butter. Add the eggs and mix until smooth. Sift the flour and baking powder together, and stir them into the egg and sugar mixture. Stir in the anise oil (and vanilla extract, if desired). Knead until the dough is smooth.

■ Divide the dough into 2 parts, then form each part into an oblong loaf 3 inches wide and 3/4 inch thick. Place the loaves in the greased pans and bake for 15 minutes, or until a cake tester inserted in the center comes out clean.

■ Remove the pans from the oven and let the loaves cool slightly. Then remove the loaves from the pans and cut them into 1-inch crosswise slices. Place the slices on the greased baking sheets and toast them for 1 to 2 minutes on the lowest shelf under the broiler, watching carefully and turning until each side is lightly browned.

Italian Creams

MAKES ABOUT
3 DOZEN

A white fudge candy.

INGREDIENTS

1 cup milk	1 teaspoon vanilla extract
3 cups sugar	3/4 cup chopped walnuts
1 1/2 teaspoons butter	

METHOD

■ Butter a large baking pan.

■ Heat the milk and 2 cups of the sugar in a large, heavy saucepan, stirring occasionally. Allow the mixture to boil gently. Add the butter.

■ While the milk mixture heats, heat the remaining sugar in a heavy skillet, stirring gently so the sugar melts without burning. When the sugar in the skillet is completely melted, remove the hot milk and sugar mixture from the heat and stir the melted sugar into it. Return the saucepan to the heat and cook, stirring gently, until the temperature reaches 234° F, or when a drop of the mixture placed in water forms a soft ball. Remove the pan from the heat, and beat the mixture by hand until it thickens. Add the vanilla extract and walnuts. Pour the candy into the buttered pan and let it cool. When it is firm, cut it into squares as you would fudge.

INDEX

COOKBOOKS BY THE CROSSING PRESS

Homestyle Cooking Series

Homestyle Mexican Cooking
By Lourdes Nichols
$16.95 • Paper • ISBN 0-89594-861-3

Homestyle Thai and Indonesian Cooking
By Sri Owen
$16.95 • Paper • ISBN 0-89594-859-1

Homestyle Italian Cooking
By Lori Carangelo
$16.95 • Paper • ISBN 0-89594-867-2

Global Cuisine

Global Grilling
Sizzling Recipes from Around the World
By Jay Solomon
$10.95 • Paper • ISBN 0-89594-666-1

Global Kitchen
*Meat and Vegetarian Recipes from Africa,
Asia and Latin America for Western Kitchens*
By Troth Wells
$16.95 • Paper • ISBN 0-89594-753-6

The World in Your Kitchen
*Vegetarian Recipes from Africa,
Asia and Latin America*
By Troth Wells
Foreword by Glenda Jackson
$16.95 • Paper • ISBN 0-89594-577-0

COOKBOOKS BY THE CROSSING PRESS

International Vegetarian Cooking
by Judy Ridgway
$14.95 • Paper • ISBN 0-89594-854-0

Island Cooking
Recipes from the Caribbean
By Dunstan Harris
$10.95 • Paper • ISBN 0-89594-400-6

Japanese Vegetarian Cooking
From Simple Soups to Sushi
By Patricia Richfield
$14.95 • Paper • ISBN 0-89594-805-2

Indian Cuisine

From Bengal to Punjab
The Cuisines of India
By Smita Chandra
$12.95 • Paper • ISBN 0-89594-509-6

The Spice Box
Vegetarian Indian Cookbook
By Manju Shivraj Singh
$12.95 • Paper • ISBN 0-89594-053-1

Taste of the Tropics
Traditional and Innovative Cooking from the Pacific and Caribbean
By Jay Solomon
$10.95 • Paper • ISBN 0-89594-533-9

Traveling Jamaica with Knife, Fork & Spoon
By Robb Walsh and Jay McCarthy
$16.95 • Paper • ISBN 0-89594-698-X

To receive a current catalog from The Crossing Press
please call toll-free, 800-777-1048.
Visit our Web site on the Internet: www. crossingpress.com